## More Advance Praise for
### *High-Tech, High-Touch Customer Service*

"Finally, a masterpiece that confronts how technology and customer service complement each other. Micah Solomon has taken a multifaceted topic and made it practical and accessible. This book is a must-read for any person or organization that wants to successfully compete in today's global economy."

—MICHAEL C. HYTER, President and Managing Partner, Global Novations

"Author Micah Solomon, a contemporary thought leader in the customer service and marketing arenas, teaches you how to preserve all that is timeless and crucial in great customer service in the midst of today's raging revolution in technology and in customer expectations. Anyone who works with customers needs to read *High-Tech, High-Touch Customer Service*."

—JARED SCOTT, Managing Partner, Red Tettemer + Partners

"In a world where even professional services risk being considered commodities, customer service is the last differentiator. *High-Tech, High-Touch Customer Service* guides us, with warmth and humor, through the steps needed to successfully merge touch and technology, building an emotional bond between provider and customer that becomes the basis of enduring relationships."

—MARK DARRALL, AIA, A2SO4 Architecture, LLC

"Micah Solomon's expertise is critical in the Financial Services industry to avoid the commoditization that technological uniformity threatens to bring. He does a masterful job of demonstrating how to create successful, valuable customer relationships with a combination of case examples and personal experience. Everyone in the financial services industry should follow Micah's advice if customer satisfaction, retention, and loyalty are part of their goals."

—AARON TALLEN, Director of Institutional Retirement Plan Services, Security Benefit

# high-tech, high-touch customer service

Inspire Timeless Loyalty in the Demanding
New World of Social Commerce

**Micah Solomon**

American Management Association
New York • Atlanta • Brussels • Chicago • Mexico City • San Francisco
Shanghai • Tokyo • Toronto • Washington, D.C.

*This publication is designed to provide accurate and authoritative information in regard to the subject matter covered. It is sold with the understanding that neither the publisher nor the author is not engaged in rendering legal, accounting, or other professional service. If legal advice or other expert assistance is required, the services of a competent professional person should be sought.*

*In a few instances, the author has concealed identifying characteristics of individuals or businesses, especially in less-than-laudatory examples.*

*Library of Congress Cataloging-in-Publication Data*

*Solomon, Micah.*
    *High-tech, high-touch customer service : inspire timeless loyalty in the demanding new world of social commerce / Micah Solomon.*
        *p.    cm.*
    *Includes index.*
    *ISBN 978-0-8144-1790-4—ISBN 0-8144-1790-6*
    *1. Customer services.    2. Customer services—Technological innovations.    3. Customer loyalty.    4. Social media.    I. Title.*
    *HF5415.5.S6219    2012*
    *658.8′12—dc23*

                                                                                    *2012001970*

**About AMA**

*American Management Association (www.amanet.org) is a world leader in talent development, advancing the skills of individuals to drive business success. Our mission is to support the goals of individuals and organizations through a complete range of products and services, including classroom and virtual seminars, webcasts, webinars, podcasts, conferences, corporate and government solutions, business books and research. AMA's approach to improving performance combines experiential learning—learning through doing—with opportunities for ongoing professional growth at every step of one's career journey.*

*Printing number*
*10    9    8    7    6    5    4    3    2    1*

# contents

# acknowledgments

**There are many people** to whom I am grateful, including Vandy, Lila, Noah, Mom, Dad, Ari, Slim, Brynda, Paul Reisler, Art, Marla, Leigh Buchanan, Jane Lindsey, Rajesh Setty, Jay Coldren, Bill Gladstone, Seth Godin, Leonardo Inghilleri, Peter Shankman, Bill Price and David Jaffe, Shep Hyken, Richard Narramore, Daniel Pink, Frank Philpot, Cathy Hirst, John Jantsch, Bob Nirkind, Rosemary Carlough, Irene Majuk, William Helms, Jenny Wesselmann, Michele Livingston, my teachers (including Eugenie Latchis Silverthorne, Philip Levine, and the late Gary McCown), Carol Tice, Pamela Keyes, Doug Boehmer, Barbara Allen, Colin Taylor, Dan Schuman, everyone at Oasis Disc Manufacturing and AVL, Jim Miller, Ann Nodei, Marybeth Grass, Steve Cunningham, Shep Shapiro, Farah Perelmuter, Kenneth Kales, Jon Mueller, everyone at 800-CEO-READ, Jared Scott, Grace Sharples Cook, Janet and Steve Wozniak, Ron Wingard, Michael Zimmerman, and of course my speaking audiences and consulting clients who teach me new things every day.

# special features

# introduction

**marshall plympton** (not his actual name, although I was tempted) is the all-too-real proprietor of an "eclectic American" restaurant near our vacation spot in the central Carolinas. Marshall's eatery has forty-seven reviews on Yelp, twelve on Google, and thirteen on TripAdvisor. The majority of these reviews are actually pretty positive.

Marshall, however, isn't satisfied with his good reviews and has no interest in learning from anything constructive in the mixed ones. Instead, he responds to even the smallest online slight with outrage. *Outrageous* outrage. Here's one example of Marshall responding on Yelp to a very mild critique:

> If any other bleepholes [except Marshall didn't type "bleepholes"] like "Jjhamle319" are thinking of coming to my restaurant, listen up: Please DON'T come. Just DON'T. I have enough work serving the rest of you people without this kind of grief. And Jjhamie319, so WHAT if your soup was cold. "Cold" is subjective. We are only three people in the kitchen, sometimes four depending on the season. Can YOU keep soup hot at YOUR house? Big bleeping deal that it was quote unquote "cold" twice. Don't come in again—make your own soup. Hope you scald your mouth.[1]

*Marshall doesn't need my book; he needs a new line of work,* far away from customers. But for the rest of you, who'd like to keep your organization free of what could be termed "Marshall Lawlessness" and learn to get along with and win over today's breed of customer, I offer this book.

Social media blundering, even in milder forms than Marshall's, is one of the potential pitfalls of engaging with customers today, but it's not the only one. And the book you're reading is not exclusively about social media, because what an organization needs in order to avoid responses that evoke our clueless Marshall is much more than nuts-and-bolts training in social media. What's needed could be more properly termed *training in humanity*. Humanity training involves:

- ▶ Understanding customers and their desires, unformed and always-shifting though they may be

- ▶ Consciously building an extraordinary company culture

- ▶ Understanding, appropriately selecting, and engaging employees

And, of course, learning the special code of technologically clued-in commerce, including social media: how to respond, when to respond, and when, in fact, to keep your mouth (terminal, actually) shut. All of which I'll cover as we move through this book.

## forearmed is fore*warmed*

It was behavioral scientist Nicolas Guégen who proved the power, literally speaking, of touch.[2] He demonstrated it definitively—and a bit creepily, I might add. His research experiments showed that giving a light touch on the arm nearly doubles your chance of getting what you want: convincing someone to join you in charity work, getting the phone number of an attractive stranger you've spotted on the street, getting the quiet newcomer in the meeting to take on a thankless project.

And most relevant to our subject, he proved that this tap can help convince a stranger to participate in a supermarket taste test and, ultimately, to buy your product. (Before we get *too* dependent on Guégen's work, I feel obliged to note that Guégen's research strays into some curious territory, such as determining, for female hitchhikers, the ideal bust size to entice a male driver to stop.[3] So I'm not going to be using the full range of his research in this book.)

Of course, we can't actually touch our customers on the arm: It's not, as far as I know, possible to do over the internet, and it's prone to misinterpretation if done in person. Yet, figuratively, we do need to touch our customers if we're going to provide memorable customer service. And touching—reaching—your customers is what this book's about.

## a light touch at just the right time

I'm going to show you how to succeed at touching customers while keeping your technological edge, as well as how to make that touch more effective *through* your technological edge. You'll also learn how to use the right technology, people, and company culture to ensure that your touch is feather light—not intrusive or more than the customer wants, and always (and only) *when* the customer wants it.

The goal in all this is to touch customers in a way that builds true customer loyalty—loyalty you can bank.

The stakes are high. Since the advent of the internet, and, most specifically, the broad use of the World Wide Web starting in the mid-1990s, there's been a dramatic transformation of the competitive landscape. The changes wrought by these new communication and distribution channels are in many ways revolutionary, and they're causing disruptions akin to those of past revolutions.

For a parallel, look at the changes of the mid-nineteenth century. During this period the stability of rural and village life was thrown into disarray due to a host of technological advances, including those making it possible to preserve and transport food. Customers could now purchase edibles from across the country or around the world: The farmer in New England who had been able to count on a captive local market for whatever would graze or grow in his stony fields was now competing against topsoil-rich Illinois and lamb-friendly New Zealand. The result was a mass abandonment of farms throughout the region. The transformation was striking: Go for a walk in the woods of New Hampshire or Vermont and you'll still see the proliferation of old stone walls and foundations that attest to the abandoned farms and homesteads of this era.[4] Or just remember your poetry. This New England exodus is the backstory of Robert Frost's stuck-in-his-ways neighbor still trying to mend a fence: He doesn't realize times have changed and the fence, at most, is now preventing runaway trees. There are no cattle to contain anymore.

You can't afford to be similarly left behind by today's transformational technologies. So many things have changed and continue to change in the world of commerce. For example, our sense of timeliness: What was plenty fast this time last year feels *draggy* now to the *very same customers* because of changing expectations brought by mobile technology, social media–induced restlessness, the incredible efficiency of vendors like Amazon.com, and other factors. It's crucial to invest brain cells, time, and money to keep up with what it takes to hold on to your customers, now that we're all playing on a global, digitally connected field.

## saying your business is "on the internet" is like saying it's "on the power grid"

And yet, and yet . . . before you go off the technological deep end and jettison all that is timeless in customer service, take at least a few shallow breaths: In today's high-tech world, where people can pay for their lattes with the wave of a smartphone, saying your business is "on the internet" is as mundane as saying it's "on the power grid." In other words, doing business in a digitally informed manner should be comfortable enough for your business that it becomes *background information*, just like having "eleckatricity and all" (as long-ago folksinger Woody Guthrie creatively spelled it out) was for earlier generations. This has two implications. First, we need to bone up on what is essential and timeless in customer service and stop being dazzled to the point of distraction by all this newfangled internet stuff. And, paradoxically, we need to realize that the internet, mobile technology, social media, and

self-service technologies of various stripes are now, with absolute final-
ity, integral to what customer service means today—and there is absolutely no turning back.

This is the tightrope I'll walk in this book. To put it another way,
I'll bring you up to speed on everything that has changed in how customers expect companies to behave, and how to stay at the forefront of
this revolution. Yet this isn't a book that throws the baby out with
the digital bathwater, written by someone who thinks the Twitterverse
comprises the entire customer service universe. This is a book that realizes that customers—how they behave and how they prefer to interact
with you—fall along a wide continuum. The breathless generalizations
and thoughtless clichés you hear every day in the technology and business press about "today's customers" are just that: generalizations and
clichés. This book will teach you how to do business in our three-
dimensional world—with customers who walk on two legs and type
with ten fingers (or, just as likely today, with two thumbs).

Our idiosyncratic researcher Guégen was right: There is one thing
all customers have in common, in this era and any other: If you learn
to emotionally touch them, through a human-friendly website, via a
correctly designed self-service kiosk, in person, or even by mail
(remember mail?), that customer *will* respond. Learning to leave the
correct imprint on a customer, whether in an initial encounter, when
the customer honors you with a repeat visit to your company, or when
she lets you know that she's upset, are key skills in this era, as in any
other. Through these abilities, your organization builds crucial brand
equity and avoids the danger of commoditization in the eyes of the
marketplace—a danger that the ever-expanding technological and
global-sourcing arms race has made more and more urgent.

## all you need to know in a rhyming nutshell

Your touch will be felt most powerfully, with the longest-lasting after-
effect, when you keep your customer's personal, specific needs and
desires in the foreground, ideally without prompting. This is what I

call *anticipatory customer service*. Here's what to strive for through people, systems, and technology, set in an admittedly dopey rhyme for easy recollection:

> If you can anticipate
> You can differentiate.
> If customers feel at home
> They're unlikely to roam.

That, in a nutshell, is how you turn customer service into a competitive advantage that will sustain your business year after year. If you can *anticipate* what your customers want, before they ask for it, even before they're aware of or can express that they desire it, they'll never feel the need to go elsewhere. Your service is *anticipatory* when:

▶ Your product or service is what your customers are looking for—specifically what they are looking for—before they have to look elsewhere or raise their voices to ask you for it

▶ Your pricing, whether high, low, or in the middle of the marketplace, fits the model customers hold mentally of what is fair

▶ You *already* know details about your specific customers that are important to them, thus giving them a sense of belonging and saving them time and the need to explain themselves *and* you take the logical but rare next step of using these details to bring your customers additional value—for example, suggesting related purchases that suit them to a *T*.

## homeward bound

If you can make your customer feel *at home*—no, not a home like my old bachelor pad with a sink full of dishes and garbage that needs to be taken out, but a magical home, like the one where, ideally speaking, your customers grew up as kids, where the lightbulbs were automatically changed and the groceries in the fridge were chosen to fit their preference, where they were missed when they went to school and welcomed back when they came home—why would they ever stray?

This homey image won't be entirely new to my readers. As discussed in *Exceptional Service, Exceptional Profit* (Inghilleri-Solomon, AMACOM 2010), this was a revelation of the Ritz-Carlton's founder, Horst Schulze, who graciously contributed to our book. Schulze, early in the days of building the Ritz-Carlton brand, working with a highly skilled team of linguists, parsed survey after survey to find out what his customers meant when they said they wanted his luxury hotels to be "just like home." Ultimately, Schulze and these language experts discerned that his guests were looking for a business that functioned like a home run by a caring parent. I have yet to find a better archetype for how a business can build a customer experience that will command true loyalty.

## where tech makes loyalty easier

Here's the great thing: Technology can make anticipation and "home-keeping" much simpler, and much easier to reap dramatic benefits from. For example, custom-tailored, *automated anticipatory messaging* (see Chapter 10) helps you respond in advance ("pre-spond," I suppose) to customer needs and would have been impossible before the digital communications revolution. *Anticipatory design* (see Chapter 4), used so extraordinarily by companies like Apple and Google, can help simplify your customer's life. Well-designed "My Account" and other *self-service technology* (see Chapter 8) has made it so many customers are willing, even eager, to do much of the work for you to keep track of their preferences and other details—information that, in turn, makes antici-patory customer service easier to pull off. Customers will let you know how to improve more directly than before if you keep your ear to your *electronic listening channels* (see Chapter 13), thus facilitating a much quicker feedback loop for future anticipatory service. And, once you delight your customers with anticipatory customer service, they can *spread the word much more quickly via social media* (see Chapters 11–13) than was ever possible in the past.

Technology, properly directed, is the faithful friend of the customer-centered company. But technology alone is almost never enough to bring a company out of the danger zone of being considered a commodity. Technology needs people—and a culture that supports those people's best efforts—to effectively direct technology to the service of emotionally touching your customers. Providing great customer service in our technologically altered world isn't a fundamentally different proposition than it was a decade ago, but it's faster. More transparent. More twitchy. Unforgiving. Viral. Magnified. But still created by, and for, people.

Since people are central on both sides of the service interaction, that's where we go first in this discussion, with a peek at today's customer. Care to join me?

## how this book is organized

This book is organized into three parts. Part One, "Timeliness and Timelessness," addresses the basics of doing customer service right, and what it looks like when you do it wrong, in any era. Part Two, "High-Tech, High-Touch Anticipatory Service," begins to address what it takes to create a true loyalty-building level of customer service: by anticipating customer needs through the right people, culture, and technology. Part Three, "The Rise of Self-Service and Social Media— And Other Seismic Shifts," extends the technological focus by covering in detail the trends of self-service, social media, and electronic customer input in general—and ways to stay ahead of competitors in these areas.

Within these sections, each chapter is followed by a Cliff's Notes– style cheat sheet for your quick review and as a memory aid (put together by me, not by those selfless experts at the actual Cliff's Notes who got you through *The Iliad*). This summary is called, inevitably, "And Your Point Is?" (If my point is *still* hard to decipher, shoot me an email at micah@micahsolomon.com or visit me at customerserviceguru.com and let me know how I can clarify it for your individual situation.)

part one

# timeliness and timelessness

# chapter 1

# today's changed customer

## making lovemaking difficult

**customer service is like making love.** I know that sounds far-fetched, but bear with me here: It takes only a minute—or two—to get the general concept, but you can gainfully invest a lifetime in mastering the details. (And you'll never get the full picture if you only practice when you're by yourself.)

Mastering the fine points of customer service is a never-ending challenge in part because customer expectations and desires change all the time. In fact, they're different now from the last time you spoke with your customer in this case, a frequent customer of yours I'll call Lorena Willis.

A bit after 10:30 on a wintry morning, one of your contact center operators answers an incoming from Lorena. Thanks to your processes, techniques, and support software, your operator, Pam Chang, has good historical data on Lorena, including what she bought from you last year (a built-in microwave and a set of professional ceramic knives) and general preferences, such as her preferred mode of shipping.

But there's a hitch: You actually *don't* know Lorena Willis anymore.

Like all of us, she's changed. She's changed since the recession. Since the internet became what seems like a 25/8 proposition. Since the explosion in popularity of mobile devices.

In what ways has Lorena likely changed? Let's take a tour through the dominant themes emerging in the marketplace—keeping our eyes trained on those that illuminate the ways your customer service may need updating.

## the most crucial customer "trends" today are individual changes

Before I become a master of all generalizations, I'm going to concede something rarely admitted in a trendspotting chapter like this one: The most important factors that have changed about Lorena, or any customer, are *individual* changes. Is she richer? Poorer? Recently single or newly married? Does she have a new pet or is she grieving for one that has died? No matter how big you grow, or want to grow, as a company, *individual* customers buy from you, not assemblages of customers, not slices of a market. Learning to treat individual customers as individuals, honoring individual preferences unique to that customer, is a key to business success. But being aware of underlying trends in the marketplace is also essential for the success of any business that relies on significant numbers of transactions and on forward-looking planning.

## customer trend #1: customers expect anticipatory technological behavior and aggregated information—instantly

My battery died recently on my aging Volvo, and with it I lost the stations that had been preset into my car radio. Afterwards, driving around manually selecting the stations I generally listen to (more or less just one *station*), I found myself irritated to have to dig up the long-forgotten instructions on how to set a radio station into memory. After a few days, I found myself thinking, "Doesn't my car *know* I want this station as a preset? I mean, I listen to it every day—the Volvo should be inviting me to add it to a 'favorites list' or some such."

But my car was manufactured in 2004, and, of course, cars didn't "think" that way in 2004. And neither did consumers. Believe me, *customers think that way now*. They expect devices—and companies—to, in effect, say, "Mr. Solomon, I note that you've been listening quite a bit to your local NPR station. Care to have me memorize it for you so you'll not have to fumble for it while you're negotiating a difficult turn?"

Customers now expect personalized, anticipatory technological behavior and aggregated information—instantly. To get a sense of how profoundly customer expectations have changed, look around. With the advent of mobile computing, a traveler can get the answers on her iDroidPhoneBerry® that the concierge or bellman or neighborhood know-it-all used to parcel out at his own rate and with varying amounts of reliability: What's a good Italian restaurant within walking distance? What subway line do I take to Dupont Circle, and which exit is best from the station? My plane just landed—in this country, do I shake hands when I meet someone of the opposite gender?

While this bears some resemblance to the model in place only a few years ago—settling into a hotel room, pulling out a laptop, fumbling around for an Ethernet cable, trying to figure out how to log on to the hotel's network—there are real differences. Specifically, the better consolidation of information. *Surfing* the net—going out on a net-spedition to *look* for stuff seems like too much work and too big a time investment for today's customers. Today, customers expect technology to bring an experience that is easier, more instantaneous, and more intuitive. Customers want to type or thumb a few keystrokes and have the information they need served up for them concierge-style based on their IP address or satellite location and other useful clues. Consider Hipmunk—which lists travel options along with warnings about long layovers and other agonies, and shows hotels with precise proximity to your actual destination. And GogoBot, where your own Facebook/ Twitter pals have already rated potential trips for you. And of course TripAdvisor, with its user-generated ratings of nearly everything in the world of travel.

A study by Accenture showed a manifestation of this trend: Customers in a retail situation often prefer to look to a smartphone for answers to simple product questions rather than working with a human clerk.[1] The smartphone answers just seem to be faster and more accurate and sometimes, sad to say, come with a little less attitude. (We'll work on this attitude part when we get to building your culture and to hiring.)

Of course, the timeline of customer expectations in general has sped up radically. In addition to mobile computing and improved connectivity, Amazon.com is one of the key factors in this—making the level of what's in stock and available overnight absolutely unprecedented. Within *minutes* of placing your order, it's likely being slapped with a shipping label at one of the Amazon.com-owned or UPS-Amazon .com–partnered warehouses in one of many strategically located places in the country.[2] (And overnight fulfillment, of course, is only the beginning. YouSendIt, for example, a rapidly growing service that allows you to send enormous files nearly instantly, sticks it to the FedExes of the world with its slogan: "Overnight? *Are you kidding?*")

## customer trend #2: shame shift and values-based buying

"Shame shift" is a term I learned from Jay Coldren, Marriott International's vice president of lifestyle brands. It's a trend that's become a significant part of today's consumer psyche.

Before the economic downturn, the pride of being able to consume in a conspicuous manner—sitting in front of a many-inch flat screen, taking the family on a summer vacation to a center of tropical opulence—was considered appropriate and enjoyable by economically comfortable customers.

Now this same behavior may be seen as crass, even rude. The attitude has shifted from pride in showing off how much we can afford to shyness about consuming too conspicuously. But—and as Pee Wee Herman would've said, it's a "big but"—there's a huge exception.

"What we're seeing now is consumption being excused by 'attached meaning,'" as Jay puts it.

What is "attached meaning"? Think of the people you know who willingly pay five bucks for a cup of coffee, provided the coffeeshop gives part of that fiver to help the rainforest. This phenomenon is significant. A study of consumer habits confirms that shoppers are becoming "more deliberate and purposeful" in their purchasing decisions.[3] "Conspicuous consumption has given way to more conscious or practical consumerism" and "rampant deal-seeking is being replaced by more purchase selectivity."

Another study shows that *87 percent of consumers in the United States believe that companies should value the interests of society* at least as much as strict business interests.[4] Customers are demanding more alignment of company values with their own, and this customer sentiment is being expressed in buying choices. John Gerzema, chief insights officer at Young & Rubicam, told *Inc.* magazine editor at large Leigh Buchanan that, according to his vast database of consumer attitudes, *71 percent* of people agree with the statement, "I make it a point to buy brands from companies whose values are similar to my own."[5]

# customer trend # 3: timelessness over trendiness

One of the notable characteristics people seek in their purchases today is "timelessness"—a desire that has emerged from the recession at full tilt.

"When you consider layoffs, downsizing, delayed raises, and reduced hours, more than half of all American workers have suffered losses," Young & Rubicam's Gerzema notes.[6] "This very real pain has

driven us to reconsider our definition of the good life. People are finding happiness in old-fashioned virtues."

Examples are everywhere: Urban and suburban women flouting
zoning regulations to raise their own hens in their side yards; the practice of "cow-pooling" (where several families join forces to share in the
purchase of a cow); or the surge in popularity of Hunter boots, the
boots that the Queen of England wears when she walks her corgis: This
footwear classic combines authentic story and excellent product and, as
a result, has caught fire. Customers are looking for old standbys that
can become hip again. A backstory—history—has become important to
the consumer. "People are looking for things that are authentic," says
interior designer and web phenomenon Maxwell Gillingham-Ryan
(apartmenttherapy.com). The drive for authenticity, according to
Gillingham-Ryan, "will resonate with people as long as we live in these
times."[7]

But we *are* living in these times, so don't be fooled into thinking
your customers will accept timelessness without timeliness. They want
the twenty-first-century version of timelessness—on a timetable that
matches the impatient standards of the digital generation. Inconve-
nienced in any way, they'll usually lose interest. For example, Restora-
tion Hardware is perfectly positioned for the timelessness trend—but it
still needs to have an iPad app and be able to deliver overnight to the
farthest reaches of its customer base. A Twinings Tea slogan nails the
ideal, uh, blend we're looking for here: "Your 15-minute break, 300
years in the making."

## customer trend #4: customer empowerment

Customers feel newly empowered in their relationships with companies. They're expecting businesses to respect that sense of empowerment—and they lash out at those that don't. They expect that your
company will make itself easy to contact and will respond to customer
comments at a high and thoughtful level. Which I suggest you do.

Because feedback *will* be offered, whether you welcome it or not. It used to be that a peeved customer might drop by your shop and give the manager an earful. Or go through an extended search to figure out the correct address for an executive high enough to make a difference, and then sit down and write an angry letter. Later, the internet brought an increased sense of empowerment, with online comment forms and the ability to send instantaneous complaint emails.

Today, those methods are looking slow and outdated. Technology has created faster, more viral ways for consumers to make their annoyance felt. Exhibit "A" here, of course, is Twitter: Anyone who has enough people reading his tweets can get a company's attention in a hurry with a cleverly or powerfully worded complaint, either within Twitter's 140 characters or via a shared link directing followers to a longer post elsewhere on the web. Not only that, but the people who see it may resend it to their *own* Twitter followers (retweet it). Before long, one person's complaint will reach enough people and elicit enough similar responses to make the company wake up and pay attention to the message of the original complainer.

Customers understand that this is empowerment at the speed of light. And they expect you to understand it too, to incorporate the empowerment expectations of customers into your problem-resolution process. In other words, understand that the playing field has flattened—or prepare to be flattened yourself. (Much more on this when we get to social media, in Chapters 11, 12, and 13.)

# customer trend #5: the greening of the customer

While the strength of the green trend will ebb and flow with time and varies in strength from customer to customer, it's a clear underlying sentiment among much of today's buying populace. And the younger the customer, the more "hooked on green"—so there's no reason to think this trend will abate as the buying power of younger consumers increases. In interacting with your customers, it's always wise to operate from the assumption that they'll have concerns relating to the environmental impact of your operation and their purchase. Those *unconcerned* with the environment will rarely be offended if you take environmental precautions, but those who *are* environmentally concerned will be upset by, for example, your business's excessive packaging, whether or not they do the favor of letting you know of their disappointment.

Awareness of environmental sensitivity should become part of the day-to-day thinking you put into customer service interactions. For instance, perhaps a particular customer who purchased a large item from you that arrived in less than perfect shape would prefer a discount rather than having a pickup and rerun of the order—because of his concern about the carbon impact of the return shipping. Or maybe your offer to throw in an additional, but not entirely needed, product as compensation for a delay will only grate rather than be appreciated.

## customer trend #6: the desire for self-service

Self-service, which includes everything from web-based e-commerce to IVR (interactive voice response telephone systems) to concierge-like self-help touch-screen menus in public spaces to passengers printing their own boarding passes at home before traveling, is a powerful trend in customer service, and companies that ignore it, pursue it reluctantly, or violate the basic laws of its implementation will be left in the dust. There are various factors driving the self-service trend: our round-the-clock lifestyle, a buying populace that is increasingly tech savvy, even in some cases the higher comfort level of socially anxious customers when doing business with machines rather than face to face or even on the phone. (The rules of doing self-service correctly are explored in depth in Chapter 8. Disregard them at your own peril.)

◆ ◆ ◆ ◆ ◆

*Yeow.* How can you keep your knowledge up to date to meet the changing needs of your customer? Especially when every business's customers are different from every other business's—and the best a chapter like this can do for you is to paint things in broad strokes?

The answer: *ask*. Once you've built true customer intimacy, as we'll spend much of this book together doing, you'll have the ultimate foothold into the future. Truly loyal customers earnestly want to share with you how their needs and wishes are changing. And how they want you to change with—and for—them.

Now, I don't mean "ask" as a pat answer. Keeping tabs on and understanding your customers is difficult, exhausting, literally endless, and often confusing. Think of the man in the *New Yorker* cartoon telling his companion while scanning the wine list, "I want Chardonnay, but I like saying 'Pinot Grigio.'" If customers willingly will buy what they don't "want" (and believe me, they do it all the time) due to some psychological drive—to impress, to try something new, for nostalgia, or even to roll particular French words like "Pinot Grigio" around on their tongues—how can you ever know on any kind of immutable basis what they really are seeking from you?

You can't really: There's no "set and forget" in customer intimacy, and that's a humbling thought. But it's also the basis of how you win the customer service game—by always asking. Always valuing empathy. Never trusting that your assessments from yesterday are sufficient for today. So, you'll have a couple of restless, even sleepless, nights keeping up. Do it well enough and your future restless nights can be in Bali, or Fenway Park . . . or wherever you choose.

## "and your point is?"

▶ You may think you know your customer, but in a sense you don't—because your customer's needs are constantly changing. The most important changes are individual (idiosyncratic to one particular customer), but it also helps to keep your eye on six trends affecting customer service:

1. Don't make your customers search for information; bring it to them—and right away. Customers today expect technology that brings an experience that is easy, instantaneous, and intuitive.

2. Conspicuous consumption is becoming acceptable only when excused by "attached meaning," leading to greater purchase selectivity. Shoppers are also demanding more alignment between a company's values and their own, believing that companies should value the interests of society as much as or more than strict business interests.

3. Customers value timelessness over trendiness: products that have a backstory. Yet don't be fooled into thinking your customers will accept timelessness without timeliness: You need to keep up with the technological times and with modern pacing.

4. Customers are feeling empowered in their relationships with companies. They expect businesses to support this sense of empowerment—and they lash out at those that don't.

5. In interacting with your customers, it's wise to operate from the assumption that they'll have concerns relating to the environmental impact of your operation.

6. Self-service is a giant trend, and companies that ignore it, pursue it reluctantly, or violate its basic laws will be left in the dust.

➤ How can you keep up your knowledge of the ever-changing needs of your customer? *Ask.*

# chapter 2

# the customer remains the same

## everything that isn't new under the sun

not to go all ecclesiastical on you, but there's an awful lot that *isn't* new under the sun when it comes to customer desires. The basic recipe for what customers want remains the same as ever. Not necessarily in the same proportions as in bygone eras (or even last month) but containing the same ingredients nonetheless.

This reality can be missed in the rush of round-the-clock tweets and RSS feeds. But while there's much that ever-advancing technology has emphasized, escalated, and intensified in customer demands, when you cut through the digital clutter, what customers require to be satisfied is, at the core, a classic: *value*. Not necessarily price, but value. (Price, of course, cuts both ways: While it's true that value can be signaled to a customer by an attractively low price, value can at times be enhanced by a high price implying prestige, safety, or sophistication.) If you want to offer value to your customers, you need to provide the following components.

# providing value: as easy as 1, 2 . . . 4

You provide value when you deliver the four components that reliably create customer satisfaction. This is the framework laid out in *Exceptional Service, Exceptional Profit*; let's revisit it here in our technologically informed context. Its importance is ever increasing.

1.  A perfect product or service

2.  Delivered in a caring, friendly manner

3.  On time (as defined by the customer)

. . . with (because any of these three elements may #FAIL)

4.  The backing of an effective problem-resolution process

Let's examine each of these in turn.

# a perfect product or service

*Perfect?* Sounds suspect: We're told from an early age that nothing and no one is perfect. If you're from a religious family, you've likely heard "Nobody's perfect except for God." (And if you're from a secular family, you may have been told—until not too long ago—something like "Nobody's perfect except for . . . Toyota.")

So let's clarify how I'm defining "perfect." I'm talking about a product or service that's designed and tested to function perfectly under reasonably foreseeable circumstances and within a reasonable product lifetime. Consider my aforementioned Volvo, which has what I estimate to be twenty-eight and a half airbags. I depend on my Volvo to keep me safe, up to a point: If I glancingly hit a street sign or telephone pole at a reasonable rate of speed, I expect to be able to walk away, maybe even drive away, from the accident. On the other hand, if someone fires a guided missile toward me through the windshield, I don't expect to be able to walk away, or walk again, period. That's not *reasonably foreseeable*, and I don't expect my Volvo to be designed to protect me from such an event. Nobody (absent the personality disordered) expects you to create products that won't ever malfunction when facing the worst of all possible worlds. But you can't design glaring defects into what you sell and still expect to satisfy your customers.

## delivered in a caring, friendly manner

Even a perfect product or service won't take you far if your customer-facing personnel are misaligned psychologically with the customers they are serving. Lack of caring delivery will sink most any perfect product or service.

. . . It can even sink your next flight—or at least your perception of it. Air travel, more than other aspects of modern life, illustrates the astonishing, disproportionate emphasis people put on caring delivery. Perhaps in no other industry do companies hold the lives of their customers as completely in their hands as do the airlines. Fortunately, the commercial airline industry and its regulators hold us in very, very safe hands: Did you know that, as I write this, there hasn't been a single commercial air transport fatality in the United States this year or last year?[1, 2]

That's an extraordinary achievement. About as close to a "perfect product" as I can imagine. And there *was* a little article in the paper about it. But the article was dwarfed by the column inches devoted to passenger frustration with customer service issues: surly flight attendants, baggage fees, overcrowding.

And this press coverage pretty accurately mirrors how passengers react. They get bent out of shape over little signs of uncaring: flights canceled with abrupt or insufficient explanation, inflexible gate agents, peanut wrappers in seatbacks. Passengers take *safety* for granted and perseverate over a lack of caring.

To quote the practical philosopher Alain de Botton, discussing British Airways in his beautifully offbeat study *A Week at the Airport,*

It was never far from Diane's [Diane Neville, trainer and supervisor for British Airways] thoughts how vulnerable her airline was to its employees' bad moods. On reaching home, a passenger would remember nothing of the plane that had not crashed or the suitcase that had arrived within minutes of the carousel's starting if, upon politely asking for a window seat, she had been brusquely admonished to be happy with whatever she was assigned—this retort stemming from a sense on the part of a member of the check-in team (perhaps discouraged by a bad head cold or a disappointing evening at a nightclub) of the humiliating and unjust nature of existence.[3]

I once heard, in a similar vein, management guru Tom Peters, a beyond-frequent flyer, give a vivid description of this paradox, based on his own experience:

> Smoke started pouring into the cabin of the small private-charter aircraft I was on, [forcing] an emergency landing. After an all-night-stay at a Holiday Inn in Buffalo, I went on to Glens Falls in another small plane the next morning.
>
> After my knees stopped shaking, was I angry? Not at all . . . (1) I'm not only not irritated by the event, but (2) I'm pleased by the pilot's good work, and (3) I only wonder that such things don't happen more often.
>
> On the other hand, there *is* an old memory that still rankles. A few months before the smoke-in-the-cabin emergency, I paid full-fare first class . . . for an American Airlines flight from Chicago to San Francisco. Yet on this four-hour, late-evening flight the crew couldn't even find a second bag of peanuts to serve. I was furious. I did a little spot on national TV about it. I wrote the chairman. Today, more than two years later, my "no second bag of peanuts" memory is clear. Translation: I can readily countenance smoke in the cabin, a life-and-death issue. But I can't countenance what I see as unspeakable neglect—i.e., no extra peanuts after forking over close to $1,000.[4]

Don't for a second get me wrong: Perfection—you need it. The perfection in question here, safety, is extremely important to me: Remember, I'm the guy who drives a car with some twenty-eight and a half airbags. But in a competitive industry, and that phrase defines all of us, not just airlines, perfection is rarely enough to hang your hat on. The softer science—care and comfort—is what lets you reach and retain a customer.

## in a timely fashion

An expectation of timeliness has been a constant and critical requirement of commerce since the dawn of the Industrial Age. In today's ultra-accelerated world of "Why do I have to wait a full three seconds for a web page to load on my Android phone?" customers are expecting speedier service than ever. No matter how otherwise perfect your product is, in the eyes of the customer it's *broken* if you deliver it late.

Worse, on-time delivery is the most movable of moving targets. What seemed speedy last year may seem snail-like today. Companies in today's marketplace need to come up with solutions that stay in step with customers' ever more extreme perception of what "in a timely fashion" means. Because if they don't, their competition will step in to fill the timeliness void. Here are a few examples of this phenomenon:

► **Marriott's 5-10-20 menu:** This menu, which Marriott has begun rolling out in casual lounges and restaurants around the country, is organized by whether the food takes five, ten, or twenty minutes to prepare, and does away with traditional groupings like appetizer, entrée, and so forth.

This is smart thinking.

Because, really, what so many business travelers, breakfasters running late, and lunch-breakers want to know is: "How long's it going to take to get my food?" Without the timings printed on the menu, the alternative is to ask the server "What's fast?" Which too often brings the server's knee-jerk reaction: "Oh, *everything's* pretty quick."

Which, of course, couldn't possibly be true. This response just means the server has no idea, or the prep time per menu item has wild variability. And who can afford to miss the boarding call for her plane, watching that "pretty fast" food fail to arrive?

► **Dude, where's my e-confirmation?** In the digital realm, when you submit a service request to a web site—for example, to cancel or update the information on your hotel reservation—how long should it take to receive a confirmation in your inbox? I'll tell you my personal answer: If an email receipt doesn't arrive within about *half a minute*, I think something has gone wrong. This impatience isn't something I'm proud of, but it's true, and it makes sense: *Today, what's been experienced once is now expected.*

► **Diet Coke advertising:** When a product has a timeliness advantage, a smart marketing department will step up to exploit it. A campaign of Diet Coke posters plastered near every possible Starbucks location asks, "Who has time to wait in line for a latte?" That's a slap at the world's most successful coffee chain, hitting in one of the few areas it may be vulnerable: There's some place on almost every block to find a Diet Coke, so do you really have time to stand in line to order coffee, and wait again while your drink's concocted?

# . . . backed up by an effective problem-resolution process

There are three moments in a customer interaction that stick out in a customer's mind above all others: first impressions, last impressions, and when things fall apart. I call this third category "service breakdowns." Service breakdowns often, unfortunately, lead to customer, communication, and, ultimately, brand-value breakdowns.

It doesn't have to be this way. You need to develop an effective problem-resolution process for these inevitable service breakdowns. This process needs to be effective at restoring whatever has broken for your customer and, more important, at restoring the customer to the state of satisfaction that existed before the breakdown took place.

If that sounds like a tall order, you're right. That's why you need to build problem resolution into your company structure, your culture, and your day-to-day thinking. It's more than worth it: Done right, you'll often bind your customers to you more closely than if the problem had been avoided in the first place.

## The Customer Experience and Human Memory

My ten-year-old daughter told me recently, apropos to amusement parks: *"I like rides that you don't like until they're over."*

The human memory is highly unreliable: Just think of the multitude of wrongful convictions based on mistaken eyewitness identifications. More to the point for service providers, it's incomplete and selective. Rather than being able to retrieve an entire experience from memory, our customers tend to retain just a mental snapshot taken during a single moment of the experience. In my daughter's case, that snapshot is taken *after* the amusement park ride ends, and brings back a sense of bravery, of getting through to the other side.

This phenomenon offers hope to customer service providers: If things go wrong for a customer initially, do a grand job of getting to the other side of that challenge and you may create a positive memory that literally supplants the initial unpleasantness.

♦ ♦ ♦ ♦ ♦

*A well-thought-out problem-resolution process starts by active "harvesting" of complaints.* Your company should have the same policy as Don Corleone in *The Godfather* and insist on hearing bad news right away. The sooner you learn about the problems customers perceive with your service or product, the faster you can take corrective action, minimize bad publicity, and turn the situation into one that brings your customer (along with your customer's online and offline friends) back to your side. Whirlpool does this with its active presence on Facebook (see

Chapter 13). Southwest, Delta, and Comcast do it by active monitoring
of Twitter—with varying degrees of success, depending on the solidity
of the organization behind the tweet. One way I do it at my company
is by allowing every email recipient (sixty thousand recipients per company email we send out) to reply directly to me if desired.

Once these customer concerns are received, through whatever
channel they come in, *your problem-resolution process needs to serve the emotional needs of your customers*. This means teaching your staff to apologize
and empathize immediately with the customer's version of the story,
sincerely and without hesitation or equivocation, saving the idea of
"right and wrong" for another time.

LEGO, for example, knows that every once in a while some of its
plastic bricks will fail to make it into one of its kits, or that one of
LEGO's youthful customers will lose a few specific bricks and become
frustrated partway through a challenging project. Where the problem
originates doesn't matter; either way, LEGO realizes that it's a problem
for the company. I became aware of this when my ten-year-old was
three quarters of the way through a challenging LEGO kit modeled on
Fallingwater, Frank Lloyd Wright's architectural masterpiece. "Hey
Dad, there are two bricks missing." Forgetting that my daughter's twice
as smart as me, I cluelessly asked, "Are you sure?" "Yes, Dad, I'm sure,"
she responded impatiently, and, of course, she proved to be right. We
looked on the web together and discovered that LEGO had a conve-
nient way to order missing pieces, gratis. Super. But what was *really*
super was the letter that came with the replacement bricks. Some highlights:

> Thanks for getting in touch with us. I'm sorry there were item(s) miss-
> ing from your new LEGO set. We try really hard to make sure all
> LEGO toys are perfect, but sometimes a faulty one sneaks through.
> Actually—controlling the quality of the toys that leave our factory is
> a big job (about seven LEGO sets are sold every second!) . . . and we
> have a whole department of experts (and machines) who test every

LEGO set before it leaves us—they even weigh every box to make sure there's nothing missing.

We'd like to get even better at catching any faulty LEGO sets, though, so *I'm passing your comments on to the team in charge of testing.* It'll help them make sure this doesn't happen again. [Emphasis mine.]

A response like this can make things better than if things hadn't gone wrong in the first place, through its well-thought-out, customer-involving approach. It brings a customer closer to the company, because now the customer has gone through this event with your company, has come out the other side, and feels that they're both on the same team. Note, especially, how the LEGO letter makes a point of including my daughter in the process of improving things at LEGO.

Expect things to go wrong. Plan for this eventuality, keeping the emotional needs of your customer central.

### Apologizing to Jimmy Kimmel for a Tsunami

Late-night talk show host Jimmy Kimmel was vacationing at the Four Seasons resort in Bora Bora (lucky for him) when the tragic Tōhoku earthquake sent a tsunami potentially heading his direction (not so lucky). Kimmel sent out terrified tweets the entire time the tsunami was approaching, with his fans shooting back snarky tweets of their own, like "Hey @jimmykimmel: If you die can I have your pizza oven???" In the end, though, Kimmel was so delighted not only by not dying but also (and maybe more so) by the service that he and his fellow Four Seasons guests received in this nerve-wracking situation, that he was inspired to write a blog post about it.

What struck Kimmel most? Four Seasons taking responsibility for—apologizing for, even—the tsunami:

> The staff of the Four Seasons took a brilliant position, one that every customer service operation should consider. They acted like the tsunami was *their fault.* They apologized at every turn. They made what

should have been a harrowing experience into the nicest picnic I've ever been on. If the Four Seasons ran FEMA, things would be very different between George Bush and Kanye West.[5]

There's a lot of power in accepting responsibility. Even when you aren't conceivably at fault.

♦ ♦ ♦ ♦ ♦

The four components of customer value, interpreted correctly for your particular customer base, will sustain you solidly. Just remember that the definitions in each of these components are built on shifting digital sands. Definitions of perfection, caring delivery, timeliness, and (when things go wrong), responsiveness of resolution are all moving targets. But make the effort to hit them right and you'll provide true customer value.

# "and your point is?"

➤ At the core, what customers require to be satisfied is timeless: value. (Value shouldn't, by the way, be confused with price.)

➤ Offer solid value and you reliably create customer satisfaction. There are four components to this:

  1. A perfect product or service

  2. Delivery in a caring, friendly manner

  3. Timeliness

  4. The backing of an effective problem-resolution process

➤ The definition of a perfect product or service offering is one that's designed and tested to function perfectly under reasonably foreseeable circumstances and within a reasonable product lifetime.

► Nobody rational expects you to create products that will never break down or malfunction in the worst of all possible worlds, but you can't design glaring defects in and expect a satisfied customer.

► Even a perfect product won't take you far if it's sunk by uncaring service. And of those two components, the importance of the "caring delivery" component can be disproportionately high. In fact, in a competitive industry, perfection is rarely enough—care and comfort are crucial to reach and retain a customer.

► No matter how close to perfect your product is, in the eyes of the customer, if it's delivered late it's broken.

► Companies need to stay in step with customers' ever-more-demanding perception of what "in a timely fashion" means. Because if they don't, their competition will.

► You need a well-thought-out, effective problem-resolution process for your inevitable service breakdowns. It needs to be effective at restoring what's broken and, more important, restoring the customer to a state of satisfaction at least as high as before the breakdown occurred. Done right, you'll often bind your customers to you even more closely than if the problem hadn't occurred at all.

► A well-thought-out problem-resolution process starts by active "harvesting" of complaints—by being eagerly open to receiving input.

► A well-thought-out problem-resolution process means learning to apologize and empathize immediately with the customer's version of the story, sincerely and without hesitation or equivocation.

# chapter 3

# timeless customer service done right— and wrong

## mastery versus catastrophe

**the ongoing revolution** in communications, connectivity, and automation, including mobile telephony, user-generated content (social media), advances in interactive and self-service technologies, and of course the internet in general, has profoundly affected how commercial interactions, including customer service, are undertaken. So have other less visible factors, such as process improvements like "lean manufacturing" (a popular management philosophy rooted in the Toyota Production System), that have been a force in many industries.[1] In light of these changes, and in consideration of all that is timeless, what does a great customer-centered company look like today? And what about its evil—or clueless—twin?

## the masterful company

The companies that are doing best by their customers in our high-tech world are created by true company builders with broad skill sets, not single-minded technologists. Whether a great company offers a techno-logical product (Apple, NetApp, Qualcomm) or not (L.L. Bean, Zap-pos, Starbucks, even your corner dry cleaner, thriving against all odds), to create long-term success, a vision of the desired *experience* needs to come before the deployment of technology.

Let's focus on a dozen characteristics that are common to masterful companies, businesses that delight their customers by providing out-standing, customer-friendly service throughout the range of their inter-actions and interfaces. How does a masterful company, high tech or otherwise, look and feel to a new or existing customer?

1. **The masterful company makes customers feel welcomed even before they physically or figuratively arrive, regardless of which channel of approach they use.** Whether on the web, via email, telephone, social media, chat, or videoconference, employees welcome customers, offering particular, intimate, and thorough knowl-edge of their location, their brand, their company.

The company frequently vets online, telephone, and other inbound experiences to ensure these are functioning and up to date; *any* channel the customer may use to approach the company has been recently checked for validity and ease of entry. This is true not only on the company's own sites but on third-party sites as well, like Google Places. (It's important to keep in mind that customers don't blame Google but rather *the merchant* if hours and location are posted incorrectly. They assume—by and large correctly—that the company has had ample opportunity to update its information and keep it current.) Negative comments on Yelp, TripAdvisor, and similar forums have been politely responded to, so the arriving customer knows that the company, even if not perfect, is at least concerned with addressing imperfections and striving to improve customer service at every turn.

2. **The company strips the customer's arrival experience of barriers that might hamper the experience.** A masterful company doggedly works to remove barriers so the entrance experience is smooth

and welcoming, whether those barriers are, legalistically speaking, its responsibility or not. In the brick-and-mortar (physical) world, for example, parking and other transportation needs of customers are considered carefully. Driving directions offered are impeccably accurate, and GPS coordinates are provided as appropriate. If parking on the street is necessary, the company provides change for meters along with reminders to feed those meters, or has valets standing by to assist. In an online "entrance," the sign-in process is streamlined. There are ideally no CAP-TCHAs (visual security challenges) that visitors are required to slog through in order to use the contact forms on the company website. Or if there are CAPTCHAs, due to spam or hacking concerns, they're accompanied by an intelligible, user-friendly audio component so people with visual disabilities, or those using your site via an itsy-bitsy smartphone keyboard, aren't locked out. A customer never has to sort through hundreds of choices to select his home country, when that could be easily determined by IP address or general knowledge of the customer base.

3. **Employees show an obvious, sincere interest in customers.** Watch for it: These employees may actually appear to have a certain visible glow, even in the most befuddling customer service situations. Employees give their *elective* efforts rather than sticking to the minimum that will keep them out of disciplinary action.

4. **The company honors its customers' desire for self-service . . . but with clearly visible escape hatches.** A customer who has opted for self-service is never left hanging without available support or an escape route, nor is he otherwise penalized for his choice. For example, retailers who offer self-checkout lines keep service attendants nearby to help customers who experience unexpected difficulties operating the register; on the phone, properly configured IVRs (interactive voice response systems) allow customers to reach a human operator *the way that they expect*—by hitting "O" or saying "agent." Online, FAQs include an option at the end of each answer for customers to receive further assistance via live support when the provided answer has failed to serve successfully.

5. **Processes, technologies, and facilities have been put in place that anticipate the customer's needs and desires.** Anticipatory service means more than hiring the right people, empathetic people who each individually take responsibility for anticipating what customers want. While the right people are central to delivering great service, it's also important to align *systems* with customers' desires—even before these desires are voiced. A company accomplishes this by first making it clear internally that its *goal* is to learn to think like customers, observe and predict their behavior, query them on their desires, and tabulate the responses so the company can anticipate what customers want next. Then it has to take the crucial next step: building this knowledge and attitude into systems, facilities, and processes.

For example: Due to a dusting of snow on the runway during a Philadelphia winter, I was delayed a couple hours on the tarmac. Not surprisingly, I missed my connection in Denver. But as I stepped off the plane in Denver, thinking I was going to need to wait in an endless line and plead my case for a rebooking, or call the 800 number and wait on hold, a gate agent from Southwest came to me, *with a sheaf of already-rebooked tickets in hand.* She asked my name and then handed me the correct one—for the very next available flight to my destination.

### Getting the Input You Need to Build Anticipatory Systems

In order for employees to build—or suggest building—systems that anticipate customers' needs, as Southwest's did, the employees, in a sense, need to have "been there, done that." Often, there's nobody like a frontline worker to observe what's going on and to figure out what needs to be fixed. So, if you keep your employees rigidly segregated from your customers, they'll never *have* a customer experience and their input will be significantly less useful. This is one of the reasons that top-rated companies offer employees free or discounted use of their own products and facilities. Four Seasons

Hotels and Resorts, for example, makes a point of allowing its employees to vacation at any of its resorts anywhere in the world, 100 percent gratis.[2] In every practical way, try to have your staff use your facilities in the same manner as customers: Have them enter through the front door, use the retail website, etc.

Nonetheless, at some point this won't be enough, and you'll need to add to the information gleaned from employee observations and from surveys (see Chapter 13) with even more detailed input from customers. In my opinion, the often-maligned customer focus group offers value here when used appropriately, as do other in-depth customer interviews. One reason for this is that your employees may come from a different background than your customers (especially if you're a luxury provider or you offer something that's specific to one stage of life) and, therefore, despite their best intention, may never be able to tell you the nuances of what is missing from the service experience you're providing.

Finally, don't forget to include input from not-yet-customers. They can help you identify the stumbling blocks you're throwing in front of first-time or would-be users. So remember to enlist *non*-customers completely unfamiliar with your business to test your processes by "shopping" you. Set specific goals for them—to complete three transactions on the mobile version of your site, find five items in your shop, etc.—and get their input on how each part of their experience went in terms of ease and enjoyment.

6. **The company keeps customer time constraints and pacing needs front and center.** The company never wastes the customer's time; masterful businesses are no-waiting zones. As a corollary of this, the pacing needs and expectations of *individual* customers are taken into account by engaged, skilled staff or well-conceived technology. For example, the time-stressed internet executive is treated differently from the leisurely tourist, based on cues received. These cues can be picked up face to face or over the telephone by an attentive human, or by

receptive software that allows users to hit "not now" for multiple options in order to cut to the chase online.

7. **The customer's emotional state and needs are paramount**. A customer isn't someone to be rushed off the phone or exclusively there to be upsold (or sold, for that matter). A customer might be calling or visiting due to temporary loneliness or for a little reassurance regarding a delivery or to ask questions about a product or service, rather than to satisfy any immediate commercial need. And yet, addressing these noncommercial desires sensitively is what will ultimately result in a profitable relationship.

8. **The company recognizes and keeps in consideration the unique realities of the customer's individual situation.** In other words, employees recognize that even if the vast majority of customer interactions follow one of several typical scenarios, each experience is unique to *that* customer *from the customer's point of view*. Responding to my keynote speech for SYTA (Student and Youth Travel Association), a tour operator in attendance explained the attitude he brought to work every day: "No matter how many times I've previously given a tour of the government sites in Washington, D.C., for example, I consciously work to remember that for this group of kids *this* tour is their first and maybe only one."

What a perfect attitude! But apart from *attitude*, how does this play out *policy-wise*? Maybe a company is proud of responding to support queries "with a goal of twelve hours." It even promotes that promise in its advertising. That's commendable—if it's a first query. But to make a customer wait twelve hours between queries when the answer to the first query was "Please tell me which operating system your computer uses and I'll get right back to you" is unacceptable—and, sadly, typical for many companies. The reality of the situation is that the company needs to shoot for a *total* of twelve hours, plus maybe a wee bit more, to resolve this issue, even though it was presented in two, rather than one, correspondence. A company with masterful customer service understands this.

9. **Standards exist—and are followed**. For example, a doorman at a great hotel is rarely blindsided by a guest trying to enter while the doorman's back is turned. How can that be? *Standards*. In this case, the standard is usually that "doormen work in teams." They simply face each other and subtly tip each other off if someone is coming from behind. They quite literally have each other's back, leading to a consistently comfortable, welcoming, hospitable experience.

10. **Something extra is standard.** For masterful companies, providing something extra is the standard throughout the customer experience. These extras are always the things the more shortsighted among a company's stakeholders want to cut first, but without them it's almost impossible to differentiate your service. When you purchase an Apple iPad, you know it's going to enable you to read e-books. Super. So does the industry-leading Kindle. And the Nook. And the Kobo. And the Sony Reader. You realize you're dealing with an exceptional company committed to the "unexpected extra" when you electronically "turn" a page on the iPad—and can literally read the letters on the flip side in reverse, "through" the digital page, as if it's a real book printed on not-quite-opaque paper. Great service in the physical world works the same way. As Horst Schulze of the Ritz-Carlton said during an earlier recession, just because times are tight doesn't mean a luxury hotel should omit special, distinguishing touches such as bouquets of flowers changed daily. Guests in that context aren't buying four walls and a ceiling but a carefully calibrated experience of the exceptional. And if they don't receive it, they're unlikely to make a point of returning.

11. **The company strives for efficiencies where appropriate, but never at the customer's expense.** Service is a unique situation as far as modern business theories of just-in-time and continuously improved efficiency go. Such manufacturing-derived techniques work for service in many *behind-the-scenes* functions; however, a significant amount of *in*efficiency, *ahead*-of-time, and *over*stocking are necessary if you want to be ready for any customer contingency. Masterful companies understand where to make use of Toyota/Lean-style systems and where they're inappropriate.

12. **The customer experience is always being improved.** As customers, we all place a certain value on consistency and familiarity when it comes to painlessly ordering or experiencing goods and services. When I order something online from a company I've visited before, I expect the menu screen to be essentially the same as I've become accustomed to—I don't want to bother with relearning the ordering protocol. Just as when I phone my heating oil company to place an order, I expect the usual protocol: to be told the current price per gallon, to be given a reasonable time frame for the delivery, and to have the delivery driver already know exactly where my fill spout is and how to get to it, without requiring me to be home at the time.

However, while customers value a feeling of consistency, a masterful company knows it always needs to improve, even to maintain that semblance of consistency, because customer expectations are continually being amplified.

In the early twentieth century, just about thirty years after the telephone was invented and greeted with awe, Marcel Proust wrote with his customary vividness about how unappreciated the phone had already become. People were treating it as an ordinary nuisance, spending more time complaining when hum or static broke up the line than on recognizing the essential wonder of this still quite new technology.[3] What was true of the telephone then is true with all aspects of the customer experience, and today the timetable in which perceptions change is much shorter than thirty years. What was a groundbreaking improvement in customer convenience last year is ho-hum today; what was timely last week feels as slow now as a dial-up modem.

A masterful company understands this and adapts and retools continually. For instance, a retail chain's simply stated goal with each new location could be: *Make this store better than the last one.* Period. This is an optimal way to improve with every store opening and also avoid endless second-guessing and regrets about past shortfalls.

♦ ♦ ♦ ♦ ♦

We'll revisit each of these twelve elements as this book progresses. Each is worth its weight in customers.

# a cameo of catastrophe: timeless service done tragically wrong

Maybe meeting these twelve benchmarks for masterful customer-serving companies doesn't sound all that daunting. Good—I'd prefer you remain undaunted. Yet there are so many opposing examples around us, the essentially anti-customer (and universally anti-employee) companies and organizations that plug along and fail to distinguish themselves from the competition, that barely meet expectations—and never exceed them, unless by chance. To be a masterful company means meeting and defeating every potentially self-destructive element, so examining these negative elements in their native form, so to speak, can be instructive. Let's invest a little time to explore what a great company *doesn't* look like. Like a fire-and-brimstone preacher's vividly painted vision of hell, taking this kind of peek into the abyss clarifies things quickly.

To pick the most basic example, I'd like you to join me for some day-to-day food shopping. Because what should be more positive and straightforward than a well financed, fully staffed, properly sited grocery store, right? Well, let's check it out. Here's a gourmet food store located in a suburban neighborhood I won't name (although, again, I find myself tempted). It's a boutique brand owned by a corporate parent, and the store couldn't hope for a better location and demographic. It's surrounded by dual-income professional households and a number of old-money families as well, whose members have high levels of education—there are four colleges within three miles, and so on.

Let's start our tour. We're in for some unsavory surprises.

***Entrance and Pre-Entrance Blunders.*** Even before we get to the store's location, it's clear that interacting with the store, or trying to, doesn't work so well. Before driving to the grocery, we check its website for directions and hours, yet come up empty-handed. Oh, but there's a live-chat button on the site, so let's try that. After an interminable two minutes, someone answers. Actually, it's unclear that it is "someone";

it feels more like some kind of auto-program because the scripts the chat spits back at us lack any personality or any direct knowledge of the store.

Giving up on the store's website, we find its location on Google Maps, as well as its hours of operation. Unfortunately, the hours posted on Google Maps and Google Places are incorrect. (In fact, they've been wrong for sixteen months, but nobody appears to have contacted Google to correct them. That, of course, can leave customers like us stranded in front of closed doors.)

Let's try to remain unfazed. On a second attempt, we arrive in the grocery store's parking lot when the store is actually open. The first noticeable obstacle is a literal one: the curb of a shopping cart corral. One of the shopping cart corral's curbs is positioned to make it all but impossible for a customer in a wheelchair to exit the adjacent handicapped parking space. For anyone shopping who has disabilities or whose friends or family are disabled, this makes a less-than-positive impression. (More in Chapter 9 on inviting in customers with disabilities.)

**Back Atcha.** Let's stroll into the store. The first unmissable visual element here is a youngish woman arranging balsamic vinegar jars on an endcap, with her backside facing squarely—make that roundly—at us. She's definitely poorly oriented for being able to greet customers and, in fact, doesn't give us a greeting. An anomaly? Unfortunately not. Walking through the store, there's nobody, even among those employees with their *front sides* oriented toward us, who will take the time or effort to acknowledge our entrance or very existence. No "Hi, how ya doin'?" No smile. Zip.

**The Emperor's New Carts.** Despite being ignored at the door, let's roll one of the store's nice-looking but top-heavy mini shopping carts through the store and pick out some items. Sounds easy enough—if you've never tried rolling hard rubber wheels on high-fashion ceramic floor tiles, the ones with uneven glazes and huge breaks between tiles to display thick, artisanal styled mortar. *Buh-dump, buh-dump, buh du-du-du-duhmp.* Sounds like artillery fire and feels jarring. Repetitive wrist strain seems to set in within a dozen yards of the entrance.

***We Make It . . . to the Checkout Counter.*** Not allowing any of this to get us down, we manage to pick out some groceries and make it to the checkout counter. At the cash register, there she is: the first human being who—strictly by virtue of functional placement and positioning—must face us directly, I mean smack dab face to face. Wait—this might be a moment of human connection!

Nope. We're not even acknowledged. The cashier indeed engages in conversation, a conversation with her fellow cashiers, and the details of an unsuccessful date last night drone on even though she has to stretch her neck sideways like a performer from Cirque du Soleil in a maneuver that directs her voice to her coworkers.

Also disheartening is how she plops our chosen items into shopping bags, dropping pungent cheese into the same bag as competingly pungent sushi, heavy items atop crushables. We might hope that by not making human contact with us, the cashier would have more attention free to achieve proper bagging technique, but it doesn't seem to work that way.

***A Floral Catastrophe.*** Sometimes the most instructive encounter you can have with an organization will occur at the edges of its operation: opening or closing time. I myself was treated to an instructive and poignant encounter when I wandered into this same gourmet store's floral shop. Come with me again, this time to observe as a fly on the wall. The hour? About 6:45 on a weekday evening (they close at 7:00, as is posted on the front door—though still not on Google). I'm here to buy some flowers, but I have just a vague idea which variety, so I'm browsing casually when, within about three minutes, the one employee there demands to know if I'm ready to buy. I tell her I'm not, yet. She keeps pressing, but offers no guidance on selection, telling me rather forcefully, "We close at seven."

With deliberate gentleness, I respond, "Actually, I think you probably are supposed to close only when the last customers leave, as long as they get *in* the door by seven." To my astonishment, she changes tone entirely, openly and innocently responding, "Really? I didn't know that. *I get in so much trouble when I punch out even a minute after seven, so I've always thought the rule was 'all customers out of the store by seven.'*"

◆ ◆ ◆ ◆ ◆

What goes into creating such a glaring example of what *not* to do? Let's take a look, working our way backward through the grocery store.

***Against Employees, Against Customers.*** My final floral cameo contains within it much of what you need to know about catastrophically anti-customer companies. They're not just anti-customer but *anti-employee*, and they end up harming customers with ill-advised policies, such as "don't punch out a minute after seven, even if this means launching your customers out the exit." Any procedures they have in place are based on a superficial and unsustainable version of trying to promote the bottom line. This approach will only backfire with unfortunate, even devastating, results.

***Without Purpose or Standards.*** Similarly but in more depth, let's look at what went wrong at the checkout register. The cashier was thinking only about her superficial *function*—to ring us up, take our money, and drop items into a bag—and not about her *purpose* in the organization, which, I'd argue, is to be the warm, human end point in an engaging and pleasant shopping experience for us, the customers. Her lack of understanding is the end result of mistraining and misleadership.

Second, there are no *standards* being followed for her particular job function. Which items to bag together, or to avoid grouping together, is one of a number of simple standards that are easy to teach and learn yet can be so damaging to a customer's experience with a business if performed improperly. Standards must be taught, measured, and reinforced. The devil is often in the unstandardized details.

Third, the cashier avoided giving even the slightest extra effort in support of her customers. In fact she pointedly avoided it—willing to risk neck strain to talk with her friends rather than pay attention to the real job at hand—which, let me reiterate, is pleasing customers not just bagging groceries. Why? It likely comes down to her not feeling invested in her company and the effective customer interactions required for its success.

***The Source of Customer-Facing Backsides and Noncommunicative Workers.*** How can an employee fail to make contact with—or even show her face to—an entering customer? How can staff member after staff member not acknowledge our presence in the store? Well, they're busy: with stocking and straightening items on the already-sparkling shelves and with the million other duties they've been assigned. Yet, just like our cashier, they haven't been tasked with their ultimate purpose: taking care of the customer. This problem can't be fully repaired until the entire *culture* of the organization is fixed. (I know that sounds disheartening, but the cure is only a few chapters ahead, in Chapters 5 through 7.)

***Bumpy Carts and Misplaced Curbs.*** What about the misdesigned, wheelchair-blocking curb and the stress-inducing ceramic floor? To some extent, this comes from "not being your own customer"—in this case, from the majority of employees parking in the employee parking lot behind the store and entering through a separate entrance. Thus, few of them discover for themselves what it's like to go in through the front entrance that customers use, see the blocked-in wheelchair parking space, etc. (The exception to this being the junior employees tasked with gathering and moving the carts back out the door as need be. If they've noticed the problems, they haven't piped up, or their input has been ignored.) It also comes from misunderstanding the reasons for doing certain things—doing them only to avoid punishment rather than for wholistic reasons. In the case of this grocery, the parking lot appears to have been striped for handicapped parking without thought or planning from the vantage point of actual customer usage, but rather for the sole purpose of meeting the minimum required by local and national ordinances and stay out of trouble. So if the owners can get away with ignoring the barriers that keep disabled customers out of their store—actually putting a curb that's impossible to roll over between them and the front door—so be it. Of course, they may be cutting out a segment of their market base: disabled people and those who care about them.

Doing things for the wrong reasons and, as a consequence, doing them poorly is often endemic in bad companies. Businesses that are inflexible in work hours tend to only get low-quality work from their employees during the rigidly enforced hours that people are on the clock.[4] Companies that are unfair or overly rigid with sick-day enforcement nearly guarantee that healthy employees will take every sick day they can get away with. Companies unavoidably end up creating hazardous workplaces when they forget the reason for safety training is *safety*, not simply trying to "keep OSHA off our asses." Ultimately, these companies that are driven only by avoiding regulatory trouble end up with bitter customers. Or likely no customers, because there's no legislation that can require anyone to shop there.

♦ ♦ ♦ ♦ ♦

Well, I know this has been a downer—an *instructional* downer, I hope, but a downer nonetheless . . , I'm glad to say we're going somewhere sunnier next: where the Apples are polished 'til they're shiny.

## "and your point is?"

Here are twelve points common to masterful companies:

1. The company welcomes customers—via whichever channel the customer approaches—even before the customer, physically or figuratively, arrives. The company constantly vets the online, telephone, and other inbound experiences of its customers.

2. Once the customer arrives, all barriers are removed that could potentially hamper the experience.

3. Employees have a sincere, overarching interest in customers.

4. The customer's desire to handle things via self-service is honored . . . but with readily available escape hatches.

5. The company has put processes, technologies, and facilities in place that anticipate the customer's needs and desires. In other words, in addition to hiring empathetic people who anticipate what customers want, the company designs its systems to be aligned with customers' desires, even before these are voiced.

6. The company keeps customer time constraints and concerns front and center in its awareness—a customer's time is never wasted. As a corollary of this, the pacing needs and expectations of individual customers are taken into account.

7. The customer's emotional state and needs are paramount. For example, the company welcomes calls from customers even when those calls don't have immediate commercial value.

8. The company recognizes and keeps in consideration the unique realities of the customer's individual situation. Even if the vast majority of customer interactions follow one of several typical scenarios, employees recognize that each experience is unique to that customer from the customer's point of view.

9. Standards exist—and are followed.

10. Something extra is standard. Without unexpected extras, it's almost impossible to differentiate your service.

11. Efficiencies are strived for where appropriate, but never at the customer's expense. A significant amount of *in*efficiency, ahead-of-time (as opposed to "just-in-time"), and *over*stocking may be necessary in order to be ready for any customer contingency.

12. The customer experience is always being improved, often via continuous improvement methods derived originally from manufacturing methodology, subject to the caveat in point number 11.

part two

# high-tech, high-touch anticipatory customer service

# chapter 4

# a google of apples a day

the art of anticipation in the modern world
of customer service

to bind customers to you through service requires what I call "The
Art of Anticipation." Most any business, some of the time, can provide
*satisfactory* customer service. And, with the help of the four-step system
laid out in Chapter 2 (perfect product, caring delivery, timeliness, and
effective problem resolution), it's a straightforward process to learn to
provide it consistently.

But *anticipatory* customer service is a different ball game, even if it's
played in the same stadium. This is where the magic happens, where
you bind customers to you and create fierce loyalty and true brand
equity.

Think about it this way: Nobody ever shouts out, "Yeehaw—I just
had an incredibly *satisfactory* customer service experience."[1] But if your
service truly anticipates your customers' desires and wishes, your customers will be well on their way to feeling they can't, or certainly don't
want to, live without you.

This key differentiator has historical validation. Starting with the
planning meetings where the original team created the Ritz-Carlton
brand and ethos that are now so widely emulated, the Ritz-Carlton

Credo has included the phrase "The Ritz-Carlton experience . . . fulfills even the *unexpressed* wishes and needs of our guests" [emphasis mine]. And every Ritz-Carlton employee since that time knows this statement by heart.

Now, let's jump forward in time from the founding of the Ritz and see what this looks like in the high-tech world, focusing primarily on the Apple customer experience. Homing in on one extraordinary company, to my mind, is a more revealing way to explore anticipatory service than rushing through a cafeteria line of superficially examined[2] examples. Why Apple? It's the current leader, by a wide margin, in high-tech customer service and experience and I have my years of involvement in Apple-related companies that help me provide a "then and now" perspective.

Apple's focus, of course, is consumer technology, spanning PCs (Macintosh laptops and desktops), "post-PCs" (iPad tablet computers), telecommunications (the iPhone), multimedia entertainment (iTunes, the iPod, Apple TV), and more—most of which we seem to be using simultaneously in the Solomon household. (An illustration involving my six-year-old son last spring shows the central position of Apple in the Solomon universe. My son's school has a weekly Silent Meeting, where these tiny kids are expected to remain silent until someone is "spiritually moved" to speak. My first-grader told me he had been moved to speak at Meeting, so I drew him out about it: "Oh, honey, what did you share at Silent Meeting this week?" His proud answer: "I stood up and told them, *'The iPad 2 will be available for purchase online, Thursday night at midnight.'* ")

## the apple store experience

When most people think about what differentiates Apple's customer service from its competitors', they think about the Apple Stores, those uniquely designed storefronts that have revolutionized technology retailing. So let's start our review of Apple there.

Anticipatory service at the Apple Store can begin for customers even before they arrive in the flesh. With the Apple Store app, Apple allows a customer to schedule an appointment so the staff will be ready to receive you properly when you arrive. (More on this in the section "A Proper Greeting at Apple" that follows) Whether or not you make use of this option, the *in-store* anticipatory customer service starts almost immediately upon entering. You're greeted promptly and heartily by a distinctively dressed and reasonably articulate individual: a technologically knowledgeable Apple representative who has the requisite passion for both computing *and* customer service excellence. This employee predominantly *listens* to you, figures out what you're there for, and personally guides you in the right direction. This type of close listening is a key to anticipating a customer's needs and desires, as I'll argue in Chapter 13. Incidentally, if you're there to pilfer, not purchase (I know *you're* not, but it happens), this employee will likely pick up on that as well; this kind of prescreening makes theft in Apple Stores less likely. (Unfortunately, the streamlined design and unusually open layout of Apple Stores does make them appealing for break-ins and holdups, although these hapless criminals tend to get nothing for their efforts, since Apple can disable stolen devices through its tracking software.)

Asked such probing follow-up questions as you're moved closer to your actual purchase, you feel heard, known, and understood. The relationship may just have started, but it seems solid and sincere, centered on you the customer, a source of comfort rather than technology-induced intimidation.

One of the more paradoxical aspects of the Apple Store experience is when this close listening leads to a store employee asking if a different item—even a less expensive one—might actually fit you better than the one you originally had in mind.[3] But this doesn't harm Apple's bottom line. Ultimately this counterintuitive approach is highly profitable. Imagine the extent to which product returns are reduced when competent customer service reps—true professionals—help you, the customer, by diplomatically challenging your preconceived, or dimly conceived, purchasing methodology until it truly matches your specific needs. And how add-on sales are increased when the level of trust is this high. Extended warrantees no longer feel like obvious rip-off bait but like solid investments. Additional "one to one" training for $99? Sign me up! The dreaded "suggestive selling"? Now it's hardly dreaded; it's even welcome—because the suggestions are *anticipatory*, they predict what you want before you would know it yourself. When you finally go home, the marketing emails you receive from Apple will be for the kinds of products and services you are actually interested in, because your personal preferences are updated while you visit.[4]

## A Proper Greeting at Apple

As I've noted, Apple is able to expect—*anticipate*—your arrival at the Apple Store if you make use of the Apple Store app, a revolutionary tool that allows customers to schedule reservations and have employees available for them personally. The results are benefits for customer and company alike. For the company, the benefit is level scheduling of demand, a Lean process principle. For customers, the app eliminates wait times and promises undivided attention, something hard to find elsewhere in retail. Then it gets even more personal. Employees often make a point of ensuring that the arriving customer's name is used *without* the customer having to reintroduce himself, even by employees who were out of earshot of the initial welcoming of the customer. The way Apple accomplishes this parallels my own published recommendations so closely[5] that I have to give Apple an A+: The first Apple employee who greets the customer discreetly passes along descriptive details, such as articles of clothing ("Jim Johnson, plaid shirt, a BlackBerry—yikes!—in side holster"), allowing other employees along the line to give a by-name greeting to the incoming customer.

## from cradle to credit card

Now, it's time to pay—and to endure the necessary evil of the exit experience. Ah, but it's not so evil at the Apple Store. The checkout comes to you: Your new retail friend brings a mobile credit card reader to where you are standing and completes the transaction on the spot. Thus, the final impression you have is as warm as the first: You're cared for every step of the way, from cradle to credit card.

♦ ♦ ♦ ♦ ♦

The Apple Store, however, isn't the end of the story for customer anticipation at Apple. In fact, it's just the beginning—the first bite, if you will. What's remarkable about Apple is that it focuses on the customer experience throughout its operation, attempting to anticipate at every step what a customer will want, whether that puts demands on a call center rep, product designer, packaging expert, or computer programmer. This is sometimes missed by analysts who look at Apple's products, or its stores, but overlook the arc that connects them. The arc that connects them is a commitment to an ethos of *anticipation*, or to phrase it the way the late Steve Jobs would, a commitment to first consider the desired customer experience and have all technological decisions follow from there. Let's look now at how this figures into the computer upgrade experience, not often considered a likely place to find an anticipatory customer experience.

## a tale of two installs

Considering I've had a continual string of personal computers since I was a teenager, you'd *think* that pulling a new Macintosh computer out of its shipping crate and getting it up and running would be second nature to me. As easy as falling off a logarithm.

Well, you'd be right . . . or you'd be wrong. It all depends on what *decade* the install took place.

**now . . .**

Last month I ordered a new Macintosh laptop to replace its older but still functioning predecessor. Why? The new model has a faster hard drive, it's lighter, and it's notably smaller overall, thus less likely to earn me the hairy eyeball from my airplane seatmates, whose tray tables I'll no longer encroach upon. So I had some attractive reasons to trade up within the Macintosh product line. And augmenting these reasons was an unspoken, compelling feature that made the decision to buy a new machine much easier: I knew it would be a piece of cake to transfer the data from my old computer and get it up and running on the new one.

First, the box lands on my porch, essentially unmarked—so much the better for its chances of actually reaching me without being illicitly diverted en route. Inside the unmarked outer box is the lovely current-generation Apple packaging, extremely easy to open, with the enclosed computer held lightly in place by perfectly sized recycled cardboard inserts.

After I turn on my new prize and dismiss an initial prompt or two, the screen asks, "Do you already have a Mac?" Answering yes, I'm offered the option of transferring the contents of my existing laptop to this new one, either directly from my old machine, which is currently upstairs and physically a bit unwieldy to work from, or from an easy-to-use, Apple-formatted backup (called a Time Machine). *Bingo!* I have one of those Time Machines, backed up just an hour earlier, in fact. My old laptop can stay ensconced for now in its pile of mess and cables, and I'll plug this tiny external-drive backup right into the new machine.

*That is nearly all there is to it.* All my transferred applications function perfectly—the serial numbers have been retained; there are no odd forward-incompatibility problems—so I'm up and running immediately. Everything is as it was on the old machine, except now it's a little bit better, with a richer-looking screen that features more pixels and a faster refresh rate, a quicker response to my every keystroke, and a better "feel" in trackpad gesture response.

As icing, a software update comes up on the screen, alerting me to the operating system changes that have occurred since my new machine left Guangdong Province in China on its way to me a few days ago. Updates that make the perfect more perfect.

As I open my email inbox, I see there are invitations from Apple, not to buy extraneous dreck but to learn how to operate my machine better. I'm offered three options here: a video tutorial, an opportunity to make an appointment at the Apple store for face-to-face instruction, or if I'd prefer to do some old-fashioned reading on my own, I'm given the appropriate links to the material.

Easy as Apple pie. In fact, it's so seamless and easy that it's deceptively unremarkable.

Unless you have memories of the way it used to be.

## . . . and then

It's 1990 or 1995. The exact year doesn't matter, because it's all the same—more or less. At least it *felt* the same to me, regardless of what incremental improvements may have been going on below the surface.

My new Macintosh desktop computer arrives from Apple, enormous and impressive looking. It's in a huge "Steal me now!" box with a bold photograph of the contents on the sides of it. (And, in fact, my order has been delayed because the first computer Apple tried to send me apparently "fell off a truck" and was never seen again.)

Why have I ordered *this* computer? Out of desperation, really, because my existing Macintosh is crashing more than three times a day, every day. I'm a hoping a new one will work better. I know at least it will be faster—it has a new processor—so the times *between* the crashes will be more productive.

I open the box, or try to. It pretty much requires a crowbar to do this without ripping the box to shreds due to the industrial-strength staples binding it together, and it takes a lot of finesse to avoid spreading fine Styrofoam bits all over the carpet. Ultimately, with some effort, I come face to face with my new adversary. The first question is whether the machine will even turn on. This sounds like an absurd concern to have about a new product; however, sometimes these computers leave the plant with software that will be discovered to be fatally flawed before the machine even reaches its destination. When that happens, you need to order, at your own initiative, a new set of startup disks to be shipped from Apple to get things working.

For the purposes of this reminiscence, let's assume my newly arrived machine turns on at the first try and I get that nice, smiling Apple face and the powerful orchestral chord that provides at least the faint hope that all is well. But here's the rub: I have no reason to trust the computer will still work for me after I get the other documents, applications, and extensions successfully transferred from my existing computer to this new one.

And this is the part I most dread. Even though Apple was, even back in the 1990s, one of the industry's more diligent companies at trying to ensure that software and hardware play well together, it's inevitably a struggle.

First, I have to decide for myself what software I even dare bring over from my old computer. Much of the software that helped me streamline my work on my prior machine is almost certain not to work on the new one—and worse, attempting to install these programs is likely to ensure this new computer fails to even reboot the next time I try it.

In any event, I have to face an absurd hurdle: The new computer doesn't believe me yet that I own this software! So, if I choose to transfer over my existing software applications—*thousands* of dollars worth of applications—it means a trip to the closet where the original serial numbers and owner's codes are stored. I'm reduced to painstakingly entering these codes, some of them more than fifteen characters long, with dozens of chances to mis-enter them. (Is that a zero or the letter *O*? Is that a lowercase *i* or a numeral one?) Then, for the verifying field in the re-registration process, I need to remember the phone number I used when I initially registered, as well as, sometimes, my historically accurate address. (Three years ago, did I use my business or home address when I registered? Or maybe my old P.O. box?)

Now I can start to find out what software works with the new machine, what doesn't, and—sometimes worst of all—what *sorta, kinda* works, until it doesn't. It's hard to exaggerate the amount of tension the process can involve; these applications and documents include my professional work—my bookkeeping, bank account records, and more. If I can't get the applications to work on the new machine, I'll have to go back to using my old, slower, crashing-three-times-a-day machine. Or I'll be forced to painstakingly export my data to another program that works with this new but exceedingly particular computer.

Throughout the process, there's no centralized help. No prompts on the screen to warn me if my software is out of date or if what I'm doing is wrong. There's certainly no hope that if I call Apple on the phone they'll be able to help me in a timely fashion. In fact, they probably won't be able to help me at all, thanks to all the third-party intellectual property that is involved, even though it was Apple's technological "improvements" that feel to me, the customer, like the cause of the new problems.

◆ ◆ ◆ ◆ ◆

This Apple of the early nineties is by no means worse than other companies; in fact, it is in many ways considerably *better*—but it has a long, long way to go. And by four in the morning, coffee-jittered out, I'm ready to chuck the whole thing for the old reliable technology of pen and paper, on a *literal* hardwood desktop—not the virtual desktop of a computer.

# bringing it all back home

There's great disparity between the customer experiences in the two scenarios I've just described, which is surprising since they emanate from the same company. Fortunately for Apple and its customers, the positive experience of masterful customer service—from safe delivery of the product to intelligent packaging to the seamless and transparent transfer of data and applications, not to mention the design enhancement and beauty of the machine—is the "after" scenario in this tale of two installs. So what exactly is *different*—what is the difference, in other words, that makes all the difference?

What Apple, present-day version, has painstakingly created over the course of years of improvement looks and feels like it comes from an entirely new world. It's elevated the dreaded process of computer upgrade to an intuitive level. Most important, it's made the process customer-centric through the *anticipation* of potential pitfalls and hazards that the customer might encounter and then built in road signs to guide the customer around those potential problems, often invisibly and always nearly effortlessly.

If you're thinking this is a product upgrade more than a customer service upgrade, you have a point. But there's nearly nothing sold today that doesn't combine service *and* product, and technology can't be left to the technologists if you want to satisfy customers. Today, great companies like Apple understand that the devices they offer are both "product" and "service" simultaneously, and that they need to build anticipation into the product itself, as well as into how it's sold and serviced.

Current-day Apple has created a remarkable tech-based version of our archetype of customer service excellence: an experience that's analogous to what a child might encounter living in a safe and secure home with loving, responsible, responsive parents. The software has been pre-checked to verify that it's the latest version—without your prompting. Apple knows this may not be your first Mac and therefore offers to transfer your personal data and preferences, without prompting. And when all is done, Apple knows you're likely to want help using your new purchase and invites you in various ways, including an invitation to visit its friendly stores, to come and see the light, rather than sit in the dark and suffer.

# "attaching" yourself to customers: gmail and more

Apple, of course, isn't the only company offering a technologically enhanced anticipatory customer experience, although Apple is one of the only ones that nails it in retail *and* in product design. Let's quickly run through a few more anticipatory tech phenomena. For an example that for many of us is as close as our fingers, consider Google's Gmail, which is stunningly anticipatory in its features, especially the intuitive features that have been introduced in the years since the original, more skeletal version was launched.[6] Try typing the word "attachment" somewhere in an email you're composing in Gmail. If you haven't actually attached a document, you get the following concerned message, sounding like something you might receive from a protective parent or mentor:

Did you mean to attach files?

*(You wrote: "see attachment" in your message, but there are no files attached. Send anyway?)*

There's also Gmail's "Don't Forget Bob" and "Got the Wrong Bob?" features. The first of these automatic watchdogs ("Don't Forget Bob") reminds you if you've forgotten someone whom you usually copy:

In addition to Dasher <Dasher@northpole.cold>_and Dancer <Dancer@northpole.cold>:

*Also include Rudolph <rednose@northpole.cold>?*

The second of these features ("Got the Wrong Bob?") will notice when you've cc'd someone who seems out of whack with your other recipients and will help you replace the "wrong Bob" with the right one:

Did you mean Charles@Chaplin.star instead of Charles@Manson.sick?

Perhaps Gmail's anticipatory *pièce de résistance*, at least for certain segments of the populace, is its "Mail Goggles" feature. This feature anticipates your inability to (soberly) send email at certain hours of the night, offering tiered math quizzes that lock up your email-sending capability until you're sober enough to get your calculations right. Clearly a Google engineer was able to channel the thinking of a snockered customer.

And nothing tops Netflix for what I call algorithm-based customer anticipation (which is even more striking in contrast to the company's periodic, publicized customer-service gaffes in other areas). Netflix's brilliant, mysterious formula for predicting the movie I next want to watch borders on clairvoyance. Netflix seems to be able to identify movies I'll enjoy with far more accuracy than my family, my friends, or professional critics ever can. This ability is based on whatever Netflix has in its magic box, ranging from my zip code to, of course, the movies I have enjoyed in the past.

It's important to realize that customers generally *enjoy* and are starting more and more to *expect* this level of anticipation in technology-driven service. The number of clicks they expect to invest before being presented with an ideal solution diminishes every month. And customer willingness for you to allow them to make—and pay for—their own mistakes is on the verge of extinction in a world where, should you somehow mistakenly try to purchase a duplicate Kindle title online, Amazon.com (another technologically anticipatory company) warns you that you've already purchased that title and *protects you from giving it money in error!* Your customer service technology and your technology-driven service processes need to be designed and operated in a manner that doesn't simply respond to your customers but actively protects them from mistakes on both your parts. Your customer service applications and procedures should act as if they're standing by the side of the specific customer you're working with, anticipating what that customer wants or needs next.

◆ ◆ ◆ ◆ ◆

Technology-based though they are, the Apple, Google, and Netflix experiences work only to the extent that these companies consider what the service experience looks like from the point of view of the customer. This ability to be customer focused is largely dependent on the culture you create and the people you hire, which is where we go next.

## "and your point is?"

Most any business, at least some of the time, can provide *satisfactory* customer service. And, by employing the four-piece framework of

1. a perfect product or service

2. delivered in a caring, friendly manner

3. on time, with

4. the backing of an effective problem-resolution process

you can even provide this on a *consistent* basis. But *anticipatory* customer service is a whole different ball game. This is how you create fierce customer loyalty—and true brand equity.

- ► If your service truly *anticipates* customers' desires and wishes, it will put customers well on their way to feeling that they can't live without you.

- ► Consider how Apple has elevated both the retail experience and the once-dreaded process of upgrading your computer to an intuitive level. It's made the process customer friendly through the *anticipation* of potential pitfalls a customer might encounter and then building road signs into the upgrade process that guide the customer around those potential problems—often invisibly and always nearly effortlessly.

▶ If you want to satisfy customers, the technology can't be left to the technologists. Today, great companies like Apple understand that they offer both "product" and "service" simultaneously, and that in order to achieve maximum customer service satisfaction, they need to build anticipatory customer service into the product itself.

▶ Customers generally *enjoy*, and more and more *expect*, a certain level of anticipation in technology-driven service. The number of clicks they expect to invest before being presented with the ideal solution diminishes every month. And their willingness to let you allow them to make—and pay for—mistakes is on the verge of extinction.

# chapter 5

# anticipatory customer service

## your culture

**i hope this news isn't too dispiriting,** but just about any business advantage you pride yourself on can be copied by a competitor. The only question is when your competitors are going to get around to it.

The *culture* of your company is the exception to this rule. Strong company cultures are overwhelmingly knockoff resistant. At last chapter's standard-bearer, Apple, insiders such as former Senior Vice President Jay Elliot credit much of the company's success in retailing to the cultural fit Apple looks for and inspires in its personnel: With a team that's totally wedded to the Apple culture, Cupertino doesn't need to sweat the imitation Apple Stores now popping up with identical furniture and Apple gear for sale.[1] Those knockoff stores will always lack staff who have the all-crucial Apple mindset, as will the stores of archrivals, such as Microsoft, which has announced that it's planning to spend heavily to increase its own retail presence. Or consider Isadore Sharp's Four Seasons Hotels and Resorts, currently regarded as one of the top five companies in *any* industry for service, after having innovated and thrived through many different eras and trends of customer service.[2]

Above all else, here's the factor to which Four Seasons founder and chairman Sharp credits the company's success:

> Over the years, we've initiated many new ideas that have been copied and are now the norm in the industry. But the one idea that our customers value the most cannot be copied: the consistent quality of our exceptional service. That service is based on a corporate culture.[3]

Why is a strong corporate culture so hard to copy? In some cases, it's a lack of knowledge. But the knowledge needed is hardly top secret, and in any event I'm going to do my best to spell it out here in short order, available for you *and* your competitors to see. So what really protects a company culture from knockoff artists? The answer is your competitors' entirely predictable inability to focus beyond the short term.

## the curse of the short-term focus

Look around and you'll see businesses focused obsessively on the short term: this month's sales target or this quarter's analyst projections. Likewise, start-ups fixate on making payroll for the first time without dipping into their line of credit. While short-term aspirations can stimulate propulsion, a short-term preoccupation can also lead to catastrophic results.

This is a *human* issue, manifested through businesses, and except when the humans in business actively strive to combat it, the results can be calamitous. We're still feeling the aftershocks from an extreme example of this—the stock market/real estate/global market calamity that started unraveling in 2008, powered by crazily configured home loans that were nearly impossible for the homeowners in question to repay. "It was fun while it lasted, at least for the financial types who profited by making dubious loans and selling them to investors,"[4] summarizes

*New York Times* reporter Gretchen Morgenson. The long list of myopic players here includes:

▶ Mortgage brokers encouraging false statements and then raking in their commissions on NINA (no-income verification, no-asset verification) loans

▶ Realtors ignoring warning signs of a bubble as they pumped up neighborhoods that were about to go bust

▶ Bond traders and ratings agencies accepting the wishful thinking and mystical math that allowed low-grade loans to magically become "as good as cash" when packaged together to be sold in tranches (slices)

▶ Congress allowing ING and others to go "regulator shopping" so that the biggest players in the mess were regulated by the smallest, weakest regulators available, which in turn courted these regulatees through promises of lax oversight, in order to increase their regulatory portfolio[5]

I'm not trying here to pointlessly joust à la Don Quixote at nationally or globally entrenched issues. I use this example only to illustrate the overwhelming ability of humans to slip into a short-term focus, and the power this gives *you* if you can pick a further focal point and start building a great company culture, one that works for you, your employees, and ultimately your customers. Your investment here will have legs, since nobody in your market is going to slow down or be patient long enough to knock it off. Take a moment to ponder Southwest Airlines and the lengthy list of predicted category killers that have tried to imitate it: United Airlines's United Shuttle, Continental Airlines's Continental Lite, Delta's Delta Express, and US Airways's Metro-Jet. What did these companies lack: Money? Name recognition? Hardly. They lacked Southwest's relentless focus on culture. And all are now bust.

# consciously building a company culture: why bother?

Building, or overhauling, a company culture isn't for the faint of heart, and it's not for those looking for a quick gain. But it's a key creator and sustainer of any company whose image and livelihood depend on customer service greatness. Here's why:

- ► The number of interactions between customers and staff is nearly infinite, the number of chances to get things wrong or right nearly innumerable. Or, if you want to try to put some numbers on it, Cornell's Center for Hospitality Research estimates that a business such as a two-hundred-and-fifty-room hotel will have some five thousand interactions between staff and guests per day.[6] There's no way someone in a leadership position can dictate every single one of those five thousand interactions. Rather, a leader's only chance to get the preponderance of these interactions right is to develop a shared cultural understanding of what needs to be done—and why.

- ► The ongoing technological revolution amplifies the problems of not having a strong culture. The best customer service approach in social media, for example, is to have people who are steeped in your culture handle the social media, and the best email responses to customers come from staff members who understand what is and isn't consonant within your culture. The risks of deviating from this are potentially catastrophic due to issues spreading on the internet like wildfire.

- ► Technological and other business realities are continually changing, even beyond the points described in this book. The changes described here are, in fact, subject to change even between now and the time of this book's publication. Yet customers continue to need to be served. Only through a strong culture will your people feel reinforced in responding to, capitalizing on, and driving forward the changes that will allow you to serve customers in the manner they desire and that will show your business in the best light.

► Employees have incredibly well-calibrated b-llsh-t detectors (to repurpose Hemingway's immortal phrase). So, cultural alignment throughout all levels of your company is the only way to avoid internal bitterness at organizational inconsistencies that look like unfairness—bitterness that ultimately can end up scalding your customers.

► What do you think's the number one complaint I hear from consulting clients at the helm of businesses? It's "I keep hearing that employees act differently—and not for the better—when I'm out of the building." With a great company culture, your employees will act consistently. They won't depend on your presence to remind them how to act. Their motivation will come from within themselves, reinforced by all those around them.

## A Culture of Saying Yes

There's an ice cream parlor forty minutes from my home—It's a delicious enough destination that the drive doesn't deter us. The ice cream's made on premises, the awnings and décor are both retro and imaginative. And the people who work there are nice.

Or nice-ish.

What they lack is a culture of saying yes. Without a culture that has yes as its default, your customers will, well, start to say no.

I discovered this shortcoming the way any other customer would: by asking for something slightly off script. In the course of paying for the ice cream I had ordered for our family and guests (a $23.40 bill), I mentioned that my kids wanted to use a gift token they'd received from their violin teacher.

The cashier's answer: "That token is only for one scoop, and every sundae you ordered was two scoops, so there's no way to apply it. Sorry."

It would've been so much better if he had ended with, rather than a "sorry," a "yes": "Absolutely, we can credit the value of a scoop." That way, an eighty-minute round trip, plus six minutes inhaling our ice cream, wouldn't have been colored by a single, unnecessary negative.

◆ ◆ ◆ ◆ ◆

The importance of building a corporate culture of yes is a straightforward concept when we're discussing the world of nostalgia-themed ice cream stores and the like. I need to concede, however, that when we get into certain corners of the automated online e-commerce world, it gets a bit less straightforward. In some businesses (eBay and its subsidiary PayPal come to mind) not everybody who visits the business is a customer. Some, sad to say, who are posing as customers are plain old (or, I should say, hypermodern) *thieves*, out to rip that business off. And a fortress mentality—in particular parts of the operation—has to rule, not just for the benefit of the company itself but for the benefit of other customers as well.

And yet . . . when a true, human customer—the kind who writes actual sentences or speaks them into the telephone—contacts a company, even one of these continually under assault companies, that contact needs to be handled by a representative from a culture of saying yes.

This balance is hard to maintain on the extreme edges of online commerce, so if we're hesitant to entirely embrace the ice cream parlor analogy here, what *does* work as a model? Well, think about a great customer-centered bank or credit union. It has security procedures: extremely good, careful procedures. But the bank doesn't repeatedly ask for ID from the customers who come in every day. It waives the overdraft fees for good customers. It has a culture of saying yes to customers. And no to the bad guys.

# you can't out-pixar pixar—but here's what you *can* do

I can't really tell you what your culture should be, but I'm going to try to anyway. Let's start with employees. Quick question: Who knows best what customers want? Upper management or the people who face customers all day? (I don't need to answer my own question here; it's a no-brainer, like asking, "Who knows best what students need: professional administrators who haven't been inside a classroom in decades or teachers who are on the front lines every day?") With that answer in mind, how should you treat your employees? *The way you want to be treated.*

This makes it pretty simple. Don't get disheartened that the physical environment you can afford to provide for them compares negatively to Pixar's offices, so dauntingly perfect it feels like a writer who gets frustrated and throws his Coke against the pristine wall would be enough to set the place crumbling.[7] Or that you're unable to offer, like Google, "20 percent time" to engineers so they can work on projects of *their own* choosing one-fifth of the time, a brave and brilliant idea that led to Gmail and other key products, but may sound like a suicidal approach for those of us less well-funded (and who *isn't* less well-funded than Google?). *Just start with treating your workers the way you want to be treated.*

Which means what? Obviously without abuse or capriciousness. Add to that with respect for—seeking out of—employee ideas, observations, and concerns. With opportunities for growth—not as a cliché to put in a press release but as a bona fide way of life in your culture—and with concern for the right of employees to have input into how their jobs and workdays are designed. Again, don't look at reports on Google's Googleplex and think, "I have to offer subsidized massages for weary employees?" That's crazy talk for the average business trying to make payroll. *Do* look at Google and think, "How can I make my campus, like theirs, friendly to workers who have children?" (Because workers *will* have children.) That's smart business and solid culture building.

The rules of being human haven't changed. Many employers have just violated them for a long time. But you can do better. Without trying to out-Pixar Pixar, out-Google Google, and out-bankrupt yourself.

## cultural friends with benefits

While I proceed to tell you how to run your business, I may as well be even more brazen and tell you what to pay your employees, because this is a part of building a culture. I'd like it if you paid them well—above market, in fact. That way, you'll never lose an employee over her need to work somewhere else to pay the bills. If you can't afford to pay above market, you need to at least pay employees an amount and in a manner that seems *fair*. In other words:

▶ Pay needs to be in line with what people in similar positions outside your company make. (Exception: if there are mitigating reasons that are understood by the employees, for example, at a bootstrapped start-up, a company going through hard times requiring a temporary sacrifice, etc.)

And . . .

▶ Pay needs to be in line with what people in similar positions/ with similar credentials/with similar quality of work *inside* your company make.[8] You can't have a successful culture based on hoping nobody sees someone else's paycheck or discusses relative pay, either within or across divisions. That just won't fly in today's ultra-connected, glassdoor.com-informed world. [If you haven't yet, spend a moment checking out www.glass door.com to hear the kind of unvarnished comments from employees that are available online now. It's the Rate My Professor of the corporate world.]

And . . .

▸ With benefits. That's right: Your employees should be your cultural friends with benefits. For those of you at larger companies, this may seem obvious, but for smaller entrepreneurs, let me tell you: Offering benefits, starting with group health insurance, is one of the best things you can do to show you care about your employees. You don't have to pay the whole cost, but you do need to facilitate its availability. It's you who have the organizational structure to make it happen, so *make it happen*. Think about it! If one of your employees contracts leukemia, what are you going to do to help him cover the treatment costs if he doesn't have health insurance—hold a bake sale or a raffle? I'm not being hypothetical or facetious here. I've seen it happen more than once, and it's not pretty.

## cultural fit, oddballs, and when not to hire

A hire, no matter how talented, who doesn't fit what you're striving to build is, simply put, not a hire. Careful here, tiger: I want to clarify emphatically that my definition of "fit" doesn't mean avoidance of oddballs— I *like* oddballs—or people who aren't the extroverts who tend to interview well. These are misuses of the concept of "fit." (When *Inc.* magazine asked me to do its "Customer Service Makeover" for a promising chain of salons that was going national, one thing that concerned me was the salon's single-minded pursuit of outgoing, bubbly personalities. "I think what you are really looking for [are] . . . people who can adjust themselves to the personality of the guest," I told them. "Everyone should be able to deal with someone who is depressed or with the no-nonsense businesswoman."[9]) Yet certain cultural-fit markers, such as the "T" for "Teamwork" in my WETCO acronym of optimal psychological traits (see Chapter 6), do require employee-to-employee people skills, and the extent to which the people you hire embody these traits will have a significant impact on your culture's ultimate success.

# positive peer pressure: the double significance of every hiring decision

One reason your hiring decisions affect the treatment of customers is obvious: the direct interactions between those you hire and your customers, not to mention employee involvement in the creation of systems and processes that aid or hinder those customers. But another reason compounds this: the peer pressure each employee exerts on other staff members, whether this pressure is negative or positive. Paying attention to this dynamic is another secret of companies with strong cultures and great hiring practices.

Pulitzer Prize–winning writer Tina Rosenberg has shown the power that positive peer pressure has had around the world in varied contexts: to combat tobacco marketing (a new youth sensibility was created where the rebellion became against corporate "brainwashing" pushing them to smoke, rather than against parents who were pushing them to abstain), to improve poor math performance in African American students (peer study groups, similar to those already in use by Asian American students, served to make learning calculus a friend-building activity), and in many other areas.[10] A similar dynamic is at work at great customer-serving companies like Apple, Southwest Airlines, and Four Seasons, even though the specifics of what the positive peer pressure represents varies widely by company:

► Where the "cool kids" are the ones who love the products and love explaining them to create new converts while, paradoxically, obsessively protecting the company's intellectual property and other advantages (Apple)

► Where everyone goes the extra mile to help customers—even to the point of gate agents slinging bags and pilots guiding wheelchairs—in a peer culture where *not* pitching in is unthinkable (Southwest)

► Where employees support each other in their support of their guests—whether that means bringing milk and cookies for kids

or working together to rescue guests in a swimming pool
during a natural disaster (Four Seasons)

## Digital Distraction Is Death: You Can't Anticipate When You're Oblivious

No matter how well hired, inspired, and trained your customer-facing staff may be, digital distraction will spell death to your very best efforts. There's no end to the good work on your part that can be undone by this dark side of new technology. Let's take a look.

Distraction means death for customer relationships, as I experienced as a guest at a recent hotel check-in. Nothing feels more deadening to a customer after an all-day, cross-continent trek than being received by a front-desk attendant who can't stop websurfing long enough to make eye contact.

It can even mean literal death. My family and I vacationed at a hotel by a swimming pool in a very famous family-oriented resort, and not one, but two shifts' worth of lifeguards were obsessing over their cell phones while going through the motions of guarding the pool.

Even if the swimmers survive in scenario number two, it's important to understand that the company's image won't. Not in these cases, nor when the captain on the wood-masted historical society schooner cruise orders a carryout meal on his cell with one hand on the ship's wheel and twenty-five passengers aboard (I was one of those passengers). Nor will it when flight attendants are cuing up text messages even if they have "nothing to do at the moment" (as I've had the misfortune to observe on three flights so far this year). So the plane didn't go down from their inattention this time. But someone's coffee cup didn't get refilled because there was no way for the texting attendants to pick up visual cues from passengers, and everyone on the plane who witnessed the episode was left with a skeevy feeling.

Episodes like this, unfortunately, really create your brand—a lot more than what has been traditionally called "marketing." The websurfing no-eye-contact check-in agent at the hotel is single-handedly undoing a brand his coworkers have worked hard to build, interaction by interaction. Customers treated this way will hardly be eager to come back—to your hotel, cruise, or airline. And—if they're anything like me—they'll spend their family vacation money anywhere other than at the resort that didn't guard their kids properly at the pool, no matter how many laughing, sun-filled images the resort's marketing department churns out for its ads and brochures.

## vendors: partners, not poison

There are people you want on your team in addition to your employees: Don't forget your vendors. You build great vendor relationships through a culture of trust and give and take. Why bother? Well, properly treated and included in your mix, vendors will save you in sticky customer situations and suggest innovations to improve future options for customers through their knowledge and effort. Question: Who knows more about the products you sell—you or your vendors? This question has no clear answer. Both knowledge bases are necessary. You have unique knowledge you've gained from your end users, but your vendors have specific product knowledge to share. The catch is, if you want that knowledge and support, you have to treat vendors like true partners.

In my manufacturing company, Oasis, some of "my" best ideas have come from vendors: "Hey, Micah, what do you think of this?"—and then something really forward-thinking is suggested to me. Maybe the concept as proposed by the vendor will lack exactly the right marketing angle, or will have a clunky name, but with mutual respect we refine the idea and we're off and running. Zappos has opened up nearly its entire system via its "extranet" to give vendors transparency on sales figures, margins, everything. It treats its vendors as partners and because of this has most-favored-nation status in the vendor community.[11]

Yet how many companies treat their vendors respectfully? An approach that aims for synergy and mutual respect is rarer than the adversarial approach, at least in the United States (this kind of trust is more common within the Japanese *Keiretsu* tradition).[12] Vendors are there to be squeezed, abused, and played against each other. You lose so much with this approach. I suggest you seek out and destroy every vestige of it in your company.

## spelling out how you treat customers, vendors, and employees

Express clearly for the record how you intend to treat people in your business dealings. That way, everything you do can be benchmarked against the standard you set, and your culture, as a consequence, can be molded and strengthened. Lay out in your core values how you want customers, employees, and vendors to be treated. Say it clearly: If your opinion is that employees and vendors should be treated as you would like to be treated, *write that down*. If there are specific ways you want customers to feel when interacting with your company—for example, if you want to give them a memorable, enjoyable, and safe experience where even their unexpressed desires are realized—*write that down*.

One way to think through the areas you want to cover, and why: An *employee* focus dramatically affects customers. Only appropriately treated, motivated, empowered, growing employees will consistently give a great experience to customers. A *vendor* focus also affects customers. Only appropriately treated vendors, acting as true partners, can come through for your customers in times of need. Finally, an obsessive *customer* focus, realized *through* your employees and vendors, becomes the icing on the cake. Articulate all these, and then get ready to *live* them. It's the best way to start building sustainable customer service results that will, in turn, sustain your company.

# how to get started building your core

Here's an actual mission statement I found covered with mildew in the closet of a defunct company, where no doubt it had been tossed within days of the brainstorming session that created it.

> We will be the supreme total quality, customer-oriented supplier to our industry of all our industry-related products while facilitating extraordinary growth and sustainable profitability at cutting-edge standards.[13]

That's not how a great company culture starts. A company's culture can begin with words, but they should represent a decision—something you actually stand for, that is then expressed in the clearest, and ideally fewest, words.

Something like this:

> We are ladies and gentlemen serving ladies and gentlemen.
> (The Ritz-Carlton's Motto)

Or like this:

> In all our interactions with our guests, customers, business associ-ates, and colleagues, we seek to deal with others as we would have them deal with us.
> (The central line in Four Seasons' "Our Goals, Our Beliefs, Our Principles")

Where should these principles come from? The two examples I've given come from strong leaders, but at disparate points in their careers and in the history of their organizations. In the first example, this state-ment formed the personal philosophy of the Ritz-Carlton's founding Chief Operating Officer, Horst Schulze, from the time he was very young, and he was thus able to bake it into the very beginning of the

Ritz-Carlton's organizational history. (It was, in fact, the topic sentence of an essay he wrote in hospitality school at age fourteen, earning Schulze, as he puts it, "the only 'A' I ever got."[14]) This kind of deep history leading to an inspirational company launch is ideal but not necessary.

## the best time to start? now.

If your company fails to have such a storied birth, don't worry. While the example from the Ritz came from a fourteen-year-old future leader, who wouldn't have his own company to captain for decades, the Four Seasons example came from a set of principles that weren't defined at Four Seasons until *many years* into the organization's existence, yet these words formed the crux of a dramatic turning point for the company that has continued to this day.[15] You should take heart in this belated transformation. If your company started as a scrappy venture and cut corners in the culture department at first (the now illustrious Four Seasons was initially a rather seat-of-the-pants operation called Four Seasons Motor Lodge, if you can imagine that!), there's no better time to start consciously building a culture than now.

### An Applecronym to Remember

To ensure that Apple's sales culture is aligned, providing customers with the experience they need while assisting the company in reaching its goals, it uses an acronym my readers may recognize as an homage to the Ritz-Carlton's Three Stages of Service, which are:

1. Warm welcome

2. Anticipation of and compliance with guest needs

3. Fond farewell

However, Apple has retooled this into a new and memorable format for its Apple-centric employees and updated the Ritz formulation with the twenty-first-century element of time urgency: "Present a solution for the customer to take home today."

*A:* Approach customers with a personalized warm welcome.

*P:* Probe politely to understand all the customer's needs.

*P:* Present a solution for the customer to take home today.

*L:* Listen for and resolve any issues or concerns.

*E:* End with a fond farewell and an invitation to return.[16]

There's great value in such memorable and *company-specific* takeaways. These slogans may sound a bit trite to outsiders (an extreme example is Southwest Airlines's use of Specially Capitalized Words and the creative spelling "Luv" in its internal documents), but that's not your concern. If they're well thought out, they quite literally serve to keep all employees on the same page—a page that can be referred to by sight or memory at any time.

Beyond your core statement (your central organizing idea, such as Four Seasons' "In all our interactions . . . we seek to deal with others as we would have them deal with us"), you'll need a bit more development and clarification to make these words more than a slogan. Do this by defining key principles in the areas that are most relevant to your business, to the people who work for it and with it, and to whom it caters. Again, brevity leads to memorability. Zappos started this process with twenty-nine core values, ultimately ending up with ten. Four Seasons, appropriately, has four, which include a brief paragraph in each of the following areas:

1. Who we are

2. How we behave

3. What we believe

4. How we succeed

The Ritz-Carlton augments its "Motto" ("We are ladies and gentlemen serving ladies and gentlemen") with a three-sentence "Credo" and a three-sentence "Employee Promise" covering the principles of how to treat guests and coworkers. In each case, these lists of values are short enough that every employee can understand, memorize, and internalize them, yet long enough to be meaningful.

## buy-in or highwayin'

It's important to achieve buy-in on your principles, but please don't read the phrase "achieve buy-in" as being entirely gentle and toothless. In all three of the companies discussed above, some stakeholders didn't buy in, so it was those *stakeholders* who had to go, not the principles. In the case of Four Seasons, Isadore Sharp worked with a few trusted employees to develop his principles. He then read his principles to all of the company's executives, receiving a reception that appears to have consisted of ear-splitting silence. (Résumés from those managers who couldn't buy in to the new principles flew out the door, by some accounts, as early as the next morning.)

While Zappos developed its core principles early and has done its best to hire in a way that's consonant with them, CEO Tony Hsieh discusses a similar fork in the road at his previous company, LinkExchange, where many of the later employees clashed with Tony's unstated but implicit core values, leading him to want to start a fresh enterprise where those core values could be made explicit and be honored. (In the case of Horst Schulze of the Ritz, he was laughed at when he tried to use his Ladies and Gentlemen Motto earlier in his career at other hotel companies[17] so it was the previous companies—not the principles—that ended up going.)

## your core values are just the start—but they *are* a start

Core values can only go so far, but make sure they go *somewhere* by taking the following six steps:

1. Write them. Simply. Briefly.
2. Accept and solicit feedback on them.

3. Reinforce them continually. I suggest that for five minutes every morning you stress one value, or an aspect of one value, at your departmental meeting. If that's too often, try weekly. But not just annually at a company picnic. Annual *anything* is the enemy of "core."

4. Make them visual. The Ritz-Carlton has "credo cards"— laminated accordion-fold cards that each employee carries during work hours. The brand's entire core beliefs, plus shared basics of guest and employee interactions, fit on that card. (Horst Schulze says people chuckled twenty years ago when he said "laminated card"; they're not laughing now.) Zappos highlights one of its core values on each box it ships out. And sometimes "visual" doesn't mean words at all. One way that FedEx shows that safety is a core value is via the orange shoulder belts in its vans: Everyone can see—from twenty-five yards away—that the driver's wearing a belt.

5. Make them the focus of orientation. That way, if safety is one of your core values and you stress this at orientation, on day two, when the new employee's coworker tells him "In this restaurant, we stack the high chairs in front of the emergency exit when we need more room to do our prepwork," [This is a real-life example—visit micahsolomon.com for a candid photo] he'll experience cognitive dissonance and work on a way to align the actions of the company with the core values they're supposed to reflect.

6. Most of all, train, support, hire, and, if necessary, use discipline to enforce what's important to you. A map is distinct from the territory that it defines, and a core values statement is similarly two-dimensional until the right people with the right attitudes bring it to life. You'll be amazed where this "map" can take you—with the right people and energetic guidance. "Maintaining a culture is like raising a teenager," says Ray Davis, President and CEO of Umpqua Bank. "You're constantly

checking in. What are you doing? Where are you going? Who are you hanging out with?"[18] And, sometimes, you have to use some tough love when that teenager is acting up in ways that don't support the culture you're working to build.

## culture meets the larger world

I want to bring your attention back to that powerful statistic from Chapter 1: 87 percent of the public [in the United States] wants companies to put as much or more emphasis on doing societal good as on doing good for themselves. In other words, *only 13 percent of your customers want to do business with a company that focuses solely on the bottom line.*

This means it's smart business when companies build into their culture what can be referred to as a "triple bottom line." Depending on the company, the specific manifestation of this could include the alliterative "People, Planet, and Profit," coined by the triple bottom line's originator, John Elkington, founder of the British consultancy Sustain-Ability, or any variation on that theme, generally including labor practices, community impact, etc. in the first column ("People" or a similar name); carbon footprint, air and water quality impact, etc. in the second ("Planet"); and sales, return on investment (ROI), and the like in a third ("Profit").

Southwest Airlines is a company that's especially proud of how the three columns of its operation interact to form what it considers an inextricable link within the broader world in which it operates. Every year Southwest issues what it calls its "OneReport: Performance-People-Planet." Southwest is the envy of its industry in the performance column, having an unprecedented thirty-seven-year streak to date of annual profits in one of the most volatile industries in the world. In the "People" column, it has a culture that values good treatment and support of employees and their families, including highly amicable labor relations in an industry where this is the exception, not the rule. ("Highly amicable" barely does the situation justice, actually: The day that long-time Southwest President Herb Kelleher retired, the pilots' union took out a full-page ad in *USA Today* to thank him for his thirty-seven-years of service. That same day, by contrast, American Airlines pilots were picketing *that* airline's annual meeting.[19]) And in the "Planet" column, its activities range from the somewhat expected (increasing the use of recycling) to the highly creative (implementing and advocating legislatively for the use of Required Navigation Performance, a type of performance-based navigation that reduces fuel use).[20] (Where "Profit" and "Planet" conflict can, of course, be a touchy issue and not as tidy as anyone would like it to be. While Southwest gets top marks in my book for the way it manages the "Profit" and "People" columns, "Planet" may have to be left open to debate. Ask anyone who watched Southwest's aggressive use of lawsuits and lobbying to stop high-speed rail in Texas, regardless of the implications for the planet of blocking that project.)

## how this plays out in a pinch: southwest's culture saves a service dog

Disney theme song notwithstanding, "Planet" is an awfully big place. So really, where a triple focus pays off most is *back home* for a company, through the admiration it receives from customers and employees. Let's look at that "back home" with Southwest. It's one thing to know in the abstract that Southwest is a company famous for its strong and service-oriented company culture. But it's even more striking when an example of this intersects in a concrete way with what you do for a living. As a public speaker and perpetual traveler myself, I was touched—although not entirely surprised—to hear that two Southwest employees had worked together to save the life of professional speaker Larry Colbert's guide dog, Banner, even though those employees had no way to know that Larry was traveling on their airline.[21, 22]

As Larry and his dog Banner arrived at the airport, a taxi ran right over Banner's leg. Although bleeding profusely, the dog never stopped working to get his master to the plane on time. Colbert was unaware of his dog's condition until two Southwest employees alerted him that Banner was standing in a pool of blood, a five-inch gash in his leg. One of these Southwest employees, Troy Anderson, got a grip on Banner's bleeding leg to stop the blood flow, carried the dog to the car, and rode with him to the veterinarian, gripping the wound all the way. (Ultimately, Banner healed entirely.)

Think about that: Troy was immersed in a culture that supports behavior like his, and Troy could predict that his management and peers would appreciate, and assist with, what he needed to do. He knew there'd be no negative repercussions if he assisted the dog—even though this meant taking work time for a taxi ride to the vet.

That's a strong customer-centered, employee-backing culture. And ultimately, it worked out in spades for Southwest, although there was no way directly to predict this. Larry Colbert *was*, indeed, a Southwest patron—in fact, a very frequent Southwest passenger. More than that, his dog Banner is pretty much a mascot for the entire NSA (National Speakers Association), many of whose 2,500 members fly more than they drive. They're not likely to forget this incident any time soon.[23]

Culture may sound like a fluffy, expensive frill. But it brings hard nosed, impossible-to-knock-off results. In times of smooth sailing, a focus on culture may not seem necessary, but as Ray Davis from Umpqua puts it, when the seas get choppy, "a strong culture . . . is a matter of survival," and there's no doubt that right now rapid technological change is churning up the seas for almost every organization.[24]

## "and your point is?"

- ► Company culture is hard for competitors to knock off because most companies have an inability to focus beyond the short term.

- ► The number of interactions at a business between customers and staff is nearly infinite, and only a strong, clear culture gives you a fighting chance of getting the preponderance of these interactions right.

▶ The current technological revolution amplifies the problems of not having the correct culture.

▶ Technological and other business realities are continually changing, and only a strong culture is going to help you respond to, capitalize on, and drive forward these changes in order to serve customers and show your business in the best light.

▶ Cultural alignment throughout the company helps avoid employee bitterness at perceived unfairness.

▶ Many business leaders say employees act differently when managers aren't looking. With a great company culture, employees will be motivated, regardless of management presence or absence.

▶ Your core values should state how customers, employees, and vendors should be treated. In my opinion, this means "the way you would like to be treated yourself."

▶ Paying your employees correctly is part of a strong culture. Pay them well, pay them in line with what people in similar positions *outside* your company make, and pay them in line with what people in similar positions/with similar credentials/with similar quality of work *inside* your company make—and don't forget to provide benefits.

▶ A hire, no matter how talented, who doesn't fit the culture you're striving to build is, simply put, not a hire.

▶ A secret of companies with strong cultures and great hiring practices is awareness of the positive peer pressure great employees can exert on each other.

▶ Only appropriately treated vendors, acting as true partners, can come through for your company and its customers in times of need.

- ▶ A company's culture can begin with words, but those words need to represent a decision—something you actually stand for, a decision then expressed in the clearest, and ideally fewest, words.

- ▶ Ensure your list of core values is short enough that every employee can understand, memorize, and internalize it, yet long enough to be meaningful.

- ▶ Only 13 percent of your customers want to do business with a company that focuses solely on the bottom line, which is a good reason to consider pursuing a "triple bottom line," like Southwest's "Performance, People, Planet."

# chapter 6

# anticipatory customer service

## your people

**once you've defined** and codified your culture, what do you need next in order to create anticipatory customer service? You need people—the right people.

Here's the first thing to know about hiring. Attitude, rather than technical skill, is what's most important in a prospective employee. Although you've probably heard this voiced before as a platitude, it's a difficult point to actually get across in our technology-obsessed age, but it's crucial. You can *teach* technical skills, at least the technical skills needed for customer service situations, to prospective employees who fall within a wide range of technical aptitude. Often, in fact, *unlearning* poorly taught technical skills is difficult, which is why master technicians and craftsmen in a variety of fields prefer to train from the ground up. The unlearning of anti-customer procedures and policies can also be a real problem when hiring from within your industry. (This issue can be compounded when you inherit employees in an existing physical facility. As Michele Livingston at service-obsessed Umpqua Bank points out, you have to make an *extra* effort in that situation to get across to legacy employees that more is changing than simply the nameplate on the door.)[1]

There's so much that's necessary in service that you *cannot* teach: As Michele's boss at Umpqua, President and CEO Ray Davis, put it facetiously, "I don't know what we could have done if we had to teach them [employees] to genuinely like people and want to be helpful or to be enthusiastic about meeting challenges. Could we send them off to class and teach them integrity and caring about the community?"[2]

My favorite discussion of what makes a service employee great comes again from the philosophical musings of Alain de Botton, discussing British Airways:

> The airline's survival depended upon qualities that the company itself could not produce or control, and was not, strictly speaking, paying for. The real origins of these qualities lay not in training courses or employee benefits but, for example, in the loving atmosphere that had reigned a quarter of a century earlier in a house in Cheshire, where two parents had brought up a future staff member with benevolence and humour—all so that today, without any thanks being given to those parents . . . he would have both the will and the wherewithal to reassure an anxious student on her way to the gate to catch BA048 to Philadelphia.[3]

Now, before you object to my parent-centric determinism, let me beat you to it by objecting myself: I know people with *wonderful* attitudes who have come from *terrible* family backgrounds. So in spite of the preceding passage, and the famous comment by Nordstrom's Bruce Nordstrom, who, when asked "Who really trains the salespeople?" quipped "Their parents do,"[4] I don't literally mean to only hire people from great family backgrounds. What I do mean is to hire people who, by the time they reach the age of employment, have come through childhood unscathed, retaining pro-customer, pro-team traits, the innate stuff that more or less can't be taught. "Most companies hire for experience and appearance, how the applicants fit the company image,"

Isadore Sharp of Four Seasons says. "We hire for attitude. We want people who like other people and are, therefore, more motivated to serve them. Competence we can teach. Attitude is ingrained."[5]

Zappos puts prospective employees through interviews and challenges that fall into two disparate categories: one for basic technical competency and the other for the softer attitude traits the company is looking for. Each of the two is given equal weight. (My suggestion: If you take this dual approach, do the "soft" part first so you don't get overly swayed, or dismayed, by what you find in the technical part of the prospect's review. You don't want to get pumped up about hiring someone for her mad technical skills and then have to muster all manner of willpower to decline that candidate for not being an attitude fit.)

Hire the right people, attitudinally. Train them, technologically. Sounds easy enough, but in all practicality, just *how* do you do that? For starters, what does the profile of the "right people" look like?

## a wet dog at petco

For customer-facing employees, the right people can be identified by my acronym "WETCO" (you'll never forget this if you picture a big wet dog at Petco):

**Warmth:** *Simple human kindness.* Warmth is perhaps the simplest and yet most fundamental of these five personality traits. In essence, it means enjoying our human commonality, flaws and all.

**Empathy:** *The ability to sense what another person is feeling.* Empathy is a step up from warmth; empathy moves beyond the plateau of liking other people and is more like reading hearts—the ability to sense what a customer needs or wants, whether or not this desire is even yet apparent to the customer.

**Teamwork:** An inclination toward *"Let's work together to make this happen"* and against *"I'd rather do it all myself."* Teamwork is a slightly paradoxical member of the WETCO group of traits. After all, customers need the help of entrepreneurially minded employees who will take charge of the situation without prodding, people who are willing to fix a problem all by themselves, if necessary. But that attitude needs to be seasoned by an inclination to favor a team approach, or your organization will soon suffer from the friction created.

**Conscientiousness:** *Detail orientation, including an ability and willingness to follow through to completion.* Conscientiousness is a key trait for successfully serving customers, and unfortunately may not always be found in those who are otherwise suited to customer service work. The quintessential "people person" may lack conscientiousness, and this one flaw can be fatal: An employee can smile, empathize, and play well with the team, but if he can't remember to follow through on the promises he made to customers, he'll kill your company image.

**Optimism:** *The ability to bounce back and to not internalize challenges.* Optimism is a necessity in customer-facing positions. Employees who can't shake off a drubbing from a customer won't last long. Support from management is, of course, important here, but the employees themselves need a positive, optimistic self-image as well to propel themselves forward in the face of daily adversity. (By the way, optimism isn't what you hire for in *every* position. We all saw some years ago what an excess of optimism in the likes of Jeffrey Skilling at Enron wrought, with his mark-to-market accounting practices, and in the folks at ratings agencies who blessed worthless mortgage-backed securities as "cash equivalent." Certainly if you're hiring a chief safety officer, you may want some healthy pessimism. But it's safe to say across the board that you need optimistic customer-facing employees, because, otherwise, customers will eventually wear your employees down to a nub.

# supernatural selection

How to select such people? An ideal approach is to match candidates to the psychological profiles of existing, successful employees. You may not have gathered this data for yourself yet, in which case you'll be dependent on an outside company to provide it. That's okay, because some of the available external tools are excellent. But you need to use your chosen methodology consistently: on every hire, rather than as the whim hits you. If you use scientific methods only sporadically you'll never know what worked and what didn't. Instead, the selectiveness of your inherently biased—that is, human—memory will trick you and you'll continue to favor unscientific, ineffective hiring patterns that will hamper your organization for years to come.

If you start with externally generated profiles, as you grow be sure to gather data specific to your company. This process isn't that complicated. Have your best performers answer profile questions and then bank these results. Have your average performers do the same, and then bank *those* results. If you show a consistently measurable difference between these two categories of employee, you have a valid test.

## trial by hire

Great companies tend to have a lengthy trial period before newly hired employees become "brand ambassadors"—that is, are ready to be foisted on the public. This is important in providing consistently great service, because how your brand is perceived is only as strong as the weakest cliché—sorry, *link*. There's no truer truism than the simile of the weak link; it's one of the unnerving truths about providing customer service. You *never* want those potentially weak links out there representing your brand, whether at the returns counter, the call center, or connected via their workstations to customers. The trial period is also important for protecting your company culture. Even in the best-handled hiring scenario, it can take ninety days to know if you have a fit. Most often, it takes that much time for the *employee* to know if there's a fit. At the Ritz-Carlton, the first twenty-one days are treated as crucial, and if you're not there for the big, transitional "Day 21," you're taken out of the work schedule. Zappos trains its prospective employees for four weeks. From week two onward, Zappos (with its unmatched dramatic flair) posts a standing offer of $2,000 cash to new hires to *quit*—Zappos would rather pay out that money up front than keep someone on who's less than committed.

## "fit" and its pitfalls

One of the terms that gets thrown about a lot today in discussions of hiring strategies—*I've* thrown it around a bit myself in the previous chapter—is "fit," as in, "How well will this candidate 'fit' into the culture of our organization/company and exemplify our brand and our mission?" It's not so easy to directly and definitively answer this question.

Nevertheless, there are ways companies try to ensure an outstanding fit between individuals and the company. At Whole Foods, after a candidate has completed a lengthy probationary period (thirty to ninety days), the candidate's coworkers *vote* to determine whether that candidate will be hired permanently, or be sent packing.[6] Zappos uses an array of unique activities and questions ("On a scale of 1 to 10, how weird are you?") in its hiring process to ensure each candidate is going to be "one of them."[7] If you didn't know how agile at hiring Whole Foods and Zappos are, you might think this sounds like a process that veers awfully close to old-fashioned hazing for membership in a fraternity or sorority. (And it's a process that at Zappos manages to sometimes involve nearly as much alcohol: "I had three vodka shots with Tony [Hsieh, Zappos's CEO] during my interview," runs one jaw-dropping comment, from their now-head of human resources, Rebecca Ratner.)[8] This is why I want to take a moment to clarify what we should mean when we talk about "fit" as it pertains to recruiting and hiring customer service professionals.

My own assessment of well-intended strategies for testing "fit" is that, in hands less capable than Zappos or Whole Foods, they can be as hit or miss as black versus red on the roulette wheel. Peer evaluations, for example, run the risk of devolving into an assessment of whether a given candidate is a good drinking buddy or a worthy World of War-craft adversary, not to mention doing an end run around the anti-discriminatory safeguards that traditional human resources procedures have evolved to support. The psychological literature here is highly cautionary: *People have an instinctive propensity to hire those who remind them of themselves*, and one has to imagine that this tendency is even greater in people who aren't trained as human resource professionals.

Properly handled, fit assessment always focuses on what is needed to be a contributing member of the organization. Anything that might stray into "hazing" territory is handled with care, forethought, and pre-cision, as it is in the application process at Southwest Airlines. South-west, which, by the way, receives more applicants per spot than Harvard, uses scenario-simulation exercises that, while certainly stress inducing, use problem solving, creative thinking, and collaboration skills similar to what may later be required in-flight.[9] Southwest also has the process and results monitored and reviewed by seasoned profession-als.[10] There's no room here for hiring by fiat or hunch.

Fit is a great concept, at least in theory, but so is what diversity experts like Global Novations' Michael Hyter call *inclusion:* "ensuring that . . . there is a fair consideration for jobs for people who happen to be different."

As Hyter explains,

> The word "fit" in the absence of that support factor can easily be misinterpreted as "being like me," instead of what the position requires. Many organizations make the mistake of assuming that those tasked with selecting new hires are equipped to do so fairly because they are nice people or good workers. But failure to ensure the selection process is based on standard criteria with trained inter-viewers can result in unintentional bias in the spirit of looking for someone who's a perceived "good fit."[11]

The incomparable wit Dorothy Parker was once asked the first thing she noticed in a person. Her answer? "Whether they're a man or a woman." Parker had a more direct connection to her subconscious than most of us, and in her quip lies the problem with "fit" in its raw state. You can substitute whatever obvious—and perhaps legally action-able—superficiality you like into Parker's line, and you'll find the unfortunate truth: Superficial differences and similarities *are* often the first things we notice. It's important to get beyond them.

# "and your point is?"

> First, hire the right people, psychologically speaking, *and then* train them on your technology.

> Hire people who, by the time they reach the age of employment, have come through childhood unscathed, retaining standards for pro-customer, pro-team traits, the innate stuff that more or less can't be taught.

> Hire your team based on the WETCO psychological traits:

>> Warmth: *Simple human kindness*

>> Empathy: *The ability to sense what another person is feeling*

>> Teamwork: *The bias against "I can do it all myself" and toward "Let's work together to make this happen."*

>> Conscientiousness: *Detail orientation, including an ability and willingness to follow through to completion*

>> Optimism: *The ability to bounce back and not internalize chal-lenges*

> A key to getting better and better at selecting successful appli-cants is, as your company grows, to develop and make use of psychological profiles that match candidates with successful employees already on your team. A test is validated if it shows a pattern of difference when taken by your existing top performers and then by your average performers.

► Great companies often have a significant trial (probationary) period before newly hired employees become "brand ambassadors."

► A trial period protects the company culture: Even in the best-handled hiring scenario, it can take ninety days for either the candidate or you to know if you have a fit.

► Be careful with peer evaluations of potential employees. Although this technique may have value, it runs the risk of devolving into an assessment of whether a given candidate is a good drinking buddy, not to mention being a potential end run around the anti-discriminatory safeguards that traditional human resources procedures have evolved to support.

► Properly handled, fit assessment focuses on what is needed to be a contributing member of the organization and is fair to those who are different. Many organizations mistakenly assume that those tasked with selecting new hires are equipped to do so fairly because they're hard workers or nice folks. But if the selection process is nonscientific and not run with the assistance of trained interviewers, it may result in unintentional exclusion of people for non-job-related differences.

# chapter 7

# sangria, sippy cups, and jesse ventura

## autonomy versus standards

in news stories that had the Twittersphere absolutely buzzing (there's no better word for it), two of America's largest casual restaurant brands—Applebee's and Olive Garden —managed, in separate incidents, to serve *alcoholic beverages* to a fifteen-month-old and a two-year-old, respectively (alcoholic margarita mix in a sippy cup to the fifteen-month-old; sangria to the two-year-old), between late March and early April 2011.[1] In a more deadly incident, one of a string of similar incidents at medical facilities, the Fresno Community Regional Medical Center in December 2010 gave Elena Silva an accidental 300-milliliter, instead of the intended, similar-looking 300-*unit* (6-milliliter), dose of the blood-thinning drug Heparin. In other words, Ms. Silva received fifty times what had been prescribed, thus making Heparin toxicity a "significant condition" contributing to her death.[2]

Does this mean the cheery service professionals at Applebee's or Olive Garden enjoy giving toddlers a buzz? Or that community hospital nurses don't care whether they're administering a lethal dose of blood thinner? Assuredly not. Rather, I believe the mixups were due to a lack of *standards*.

The kids got the booze, I'll bet, because the restaurants lacked appropriate standards for how to store and administer similar, mixup-prone drinks. The hospital apparently overdosed Ms. Silva because it hadn't worked out standards for how to distinguish similar sounding, but very different, dosages.

## patting down jesse ventura

By January 2011, former Minnesota governor, Navy Seal, and professional wrestler Jesse Ventura was fed up. Security alarms had been ringing for him in airports ever since his artificial hip replacement surgery in 2008, leading to full-body scans and pat-down body searches. When Ventura tired of this extra, intimate attention, he filed suit against the Department of Homeland Security, asking a federal judge to issue an immediate injunction against "warrantless and suspicionless" searches.

This seems an unfortunate and disconnected customer service scenario, regardless of where you come down on the constitutional merits of Ventura's case (and, in fact, as we go to press, Ventura's case has been thrown out for "lack of jurisdiction"). It seems clear, even self-evident, that former U.S. governors, even former-wrestler-former-governors with-oversized-personalities-and-weakness-for-conspiracy-theories, are unlikely to present a risk of terrorist activity. You could argue that back when Mr. Ventura was Minnesota's highest elected official, he had the means at his disposal to wreak more havoc than he's likely to accomplish today taking a workaday commercial flight.

It's a simple matter of record that Ventura sets off metal detectors because of his titanium hip implant. So why's he being forced to undergo full-body scans or pat-downs at the airport, two to three times a week, on the nonbasis that he's "setting off the alarm," which, among other downsides, would seem to be a colossal waste of time for the Transportation Security Administration (TSA)?

One word: The people who work in the airports lack *autonomy.* Without autonomy, they not only can't give fantastic customer service;

they can't even give reasonable baseline customer service. It's against the rules.

## Beating Little Kids at Chess

When I watch employees refusing to give way to customers in disputes over small charges, rushing shoppers out the door when it's closing time, and engaging in a thousand other petty, by-the-book behaviors, it troubles me because it shows such an obvious failure of leadership, a management that has discouraged pro-customer autonomy and failed to help employees understand their purpose in the organization. What's going on here is that someone has built or, as likely, allowed by default a company that functions the way you teach little kids to play chess.

You know how little kids are taught to play chess? You tell them a pawn's worth a dollar, a knight three dollars, a rook, five dollars, a queen, eight bucks. This, up to a point, is smart, teaching kids what adult chess players instinctively know about the relative value of pieces. But the flaw in the system becomes quickly obvious and makes it embarrassingly easy to wallop kids at chess if this is all they know. A kid might gleefully proclaim in temporary triumph, "Heh, heh, heh, I've got twenty-five bucks worth of your pieces," but you'll be able to calmly and cold-bloodedly reply, "Well, yeah, that's true, but . . . checkmate, buddy."

It's hard, when you're taught to play chess this way, to understand the concept that the king has no definable value because it has *infinite* value. Likewise, until an employee is taught her relation to the organization's ultimate goals, the same is true, with the *customer* standing in for the chess king. If your employees don't understand their purpose in your organization and have the power and encouragement to act autonomously to support it—sacrificing a few pawns, so to speak, when necessary to protect the customer— you'll lose the game, checkmated by customers who defect.

# the case for autonomy in customer service work

The case for giving employees autonomy in how to carry out their work has been backed up for half a century by psychological and management research. It may surprise you just how strong the case is—until you look in the mirror and think about what *you* would require to do great work face to face with customers every day.

Why autonomy? First off, people need a reason to wake up in the morning—and "they pay me" is hardly the ideal alarm clock. Think about it this way: Let's assume an employer pays approximately the same wage as competing employers do. But the employer also prescribes exactly how the job should be done, when it should be done, and where it should be done. Does this employer's approximately-the-same-as-everyone-else's wage really carry the day in this situation? Unlikely. An employee with half a brain (and, by and large, that's the minimum cranial content to look for in an employee) will sprint to any employer offering more freedom, freedom that includes:

> ▶ Flexibility in *when* the job gets done (don't tell me that parents who need to work an unconventional schedule are lesser workers; it just ain't true).[3]

> ▶ Even more important, flexibility in *how* the job gets done: both on a day-to-day basis and in having a part in *designing* the overall structure of the work activities. *This is an ethical imperative.* If you don't involve people in designing the jobs to which they devote their waking hours, you're using employees as mere tools, for their labor. Even though you're paying them, this kind of using of people is unconscionable.

Second, a company needs the ability to respond to the unpredictable, ever changing, intensely individual, nuanced desires of customers. Remember our statistic from Cornell's Center for Hospitality Research: There are an estimated five thousand customer/employee touch points every day in a business such as a moderate-sized hotel. There may be fewer touch points in your business, or, heaven help you, there may be more. To handle each of those touch points correctly requires an exceeding amount of psychological and intellectual flexibility, which will be hindered when employees know that management puts primary value on conformity. While many companies *speak* of employee empowerment, they tend to *compensate* and allocate pats on the back differently: Did an employee make the numbers this month (even if he had to finesse the books by pushing bad events to next month)? Did he get everything—sorta—shipped on time (even if it means he didn't take that extra minute to verify a shipping address and save the customer a lot of grief)? Did the employee get customers off the phone in the call center "on time" (even though lingering longer could have led to a greater potential bond with the company)?

Employees selected, oriented, and reinforced properly, surrounded by peers of the same caliber, will thrive when given significant autonomy. Otherwise, they'll wither. There are dozens of studies to support this, inside and outside of business life.[4]

You *want* customer relations to be on the shoulders of your employees. But as long as you're defining every little thing, and rewarding/punishing based on seemingly arbitrary and thus, inevitably, gamed criteria, you won't get them to carry that responsibility. Their viewpoint will soon resemble the jaded flight attendant's attitude on a big, legacy carrier who told me the other day, "The more emphatically Management comes up with new i's to dot and t's for me to cross, the less seriously I take them. I know these rules will be gone within the year, and a new group of regs will take their place."

## The Spitting Image of a Great Employee

The range of how much or how little a single employee can contribute to an organization and its customers is as broad as the range of human possibility. I think of someone from the world of science, physiologist Ivan Pavlov, as the exemplar of this—the spitting image, as it were.

Pavlov's research was *supposed* to be limited to an analysis of the saliva of dogs *after* they were fed. It was outside Pavlov's purview to even notice that the dogs salivated *in advance* of the food being delivered. In fact, by making note of this unexpected phenomenon, he made his job messier, the experiment less straightforward. Yet because Pavlov was a curious fellow, whose elective efforts had been unlocked, he changed the nature of the experiment and discovered the concept of the conditioned reflex—and a name for himself that still, well, rings a bell.

How do you develop your employees into game changers like Pavlov, unlocking their elective efforts? This is a big question, but the answer starts the moment you hire a new employee. This is the time—during the *dis*orienting "orientation" period—when you can make the biggest strides, by ensuring that every employee immediately understands her underlying purpose in your organization and appreciates its importance to the company and its leaders.

An employee has both a purpose—the reason why the job exists—and a function—her day-to-day job responsibilities. For example, in a health-care setting, "to create successful medical outcomes and hospitable human experiences for our patients" might be the employee purpose. "To change linens," by contrast, might be that same employee's function. A properly trained and managed employee in this setting will know—and be empowered—to stop changing linens if creating successful medical outcomes or being hospitable requires a different action at the moment.

Creating such an employee will be an ongoing process but is best begun at this new-employee orientation, which should be led by someone at a very high level in the company (the CEO or someone whose outlook has been personally molded by the CEO). During the orientation, the purpose of the employee should be stressed, while making it clear that she will be *celebrated* for rising to her purpose in the organization, not scolded for being a few short in the number of linens changed.

# the need for standards

Standards help ensure that every part of your service reflects the best way your company knows to perform it—a prescription that your autonomously performing employees can then feel free to adapt to suit the needs and wishes, expressed or unexpressed, of the customers they're actually facing at the moment.

The summary statement for a standard should briefly include all three points below:

1. Why the service is of *value* (why we're doing this in the first place)

2. The *emotional response* we're aiming to have the customer feel

3. The expected *way* to accomplish the service

Point three should be formulated in a manner that allows judgment and discretion to be used in all but mission-critical (Heparin dosing and alcohol-in-sippy-cup) situations.

What follows is a practical example of how a company might summarize a single standard:

▶   We answer all web-form queries in a speedy, personable, non-automated fashion that assists and reassures, binding the customer or prospective customer to our company on the first response.

▶   The response time will be within thirty-five minutes.

▶   The initial answer provided will either be complete or, if that's not possible, will couple a partial, brief answer with a promise of a comprehensive future answer within a specified time frame. In that case, expert assistance will be requested internally, but the initial respondent will own the follow-up until completed to the customer's satisfaction.

## standards and autonomy: the hybrid path

In many contexts, when asked where I stand on employee autonomy versus the enforcement of standards, my one-sentence response is "In most situations, I favor standards accompanied by the reasoning behind them and autonomy in how they're carried out." It doesn't work so well, continuing with the example of the web-form response standard, to tell an employee to "answer customer queries any time you want," because answering customer queries promptly is a crucial part of giving great customer service; it can't be left to this level of potential variability. Yet it also doesn't work to say to an employee, "You have to hurry and check this function off your list, or you're in trouble." You'll end up with cursory replies, as the employee misapprehends the reason he's responding, which now becomes not to take care of the customer, but because he's checking something off a list to avoid angering his boss.

This is why, for many situations, the hybrid path I suggest is the correct one. Explain your reasoning to employees: "We need to answer customer inquiries faster than anyone else, because our studies, last undertaken fourteen months ago, demonstrate this as one of the top five controllable factors in making a sale. The response needs to be friendly and professional for that reason as well."

Then, define any unclear terminology:

- ► "Faster than anyone else" means within two hours for an initial query, and within fifteen minutes for a follow-up query related to the initial query.

- ► "Friendly and professional" means to "use your best judgment" but also to "avoid the following list of phrases and consider the substitutes listed below instead."

Finally, you need to measure and, as needed, reinforce the standards.

The next time you see reports about companies that are ostensibly "all autonomy," look a little closer. Nordstrom, for example, is often reported to have no employee manual other than the single phrase "use your best judgment at all times." This is not entirely accurate: Nordstrom is a company supported by rigorously maintained standards and training. Or look at Zappos's reported social media policy of "be real and use your best judgment."[5] This is indeed its policy—to an extent. But only to an extent: After all, it's a publicly traded company and would be at significant risk without the standards it has implemented to protect against the untoward release of information.[6]

Employee autonomy—"using your best judgment"—is extremely important to delivering Nordstrom-quality customer service. But it mostly comes into play on the more complex and unpredictable tasks, of which there are many: selecting the items for a customer's wardrobe makeover, walking the line between honesty and not insulting a customer when she's trying on clothes, finding ways to go the extra mile for a customer. All of these tasks require an enormous amount of autonomy to succeed and a properly hired and trained staff to make use of that autonomy. For example, do you know who's legally responsible if a common carrier (UPS, DHL, FedEx) leaves your Nordstrom delivery in the rain and your $200 dress shoes are ruined because you pre-signed that it was OK to leave the package? Well, it might be you or it might be the common carrier, but it's *absolutely not* Nordstrom. Yet, when this happened to me, not for an *instant* did my salesperson[7] consider saying "You need to file a claim with the truckers." She said, "I'm so incredibly sorry that happened, and I'm bringing over a brand new pair of shoes—will you be home in forty-five minutes?"

But at the same time, many things at Nordstrom and other great companies depend on *standards*. For instance, paging in a Nordstrom store is superior to the way it's done most anywhere else. But not because employees autonomously, spontaneously decide to do it better each time they page, but because someone at Nordstrom thought through what a paging system should sound like from a customer's perspective and then standardized it. Reworking the idea of a paging system to put what a customer would want to experience (less auditory clutter in the store's soundscape) at the center, Nordstrom eliminated all mention of where and whom its paged employee is to call. All you hear is a single statement of the employee's name: "Jamie Johnson." [How can this work? The employee calls in to a central number, states her name, and is directed to the appropriate extension by a professional operator.]

## Systems and Smiles

Carl Sewell long ago titled a chapter "Systems, Not Smiles" in his classic book *Customers for Life.* He explained his point like this: If the food in a restaurant is lousy, no matter how much the staff smiles and apologizes for it, you'll likely not eat there again.[8]

Of course, Carl's *kind of* right. But the flip side is that without those smiles, nobody wants the service experience in the first place. As restaurateur Danny Meyer in contrast puts it, the two things people want from the hospitality experience are a sense of acknowledgment and, on returning, a sense of being remembered. Both of which, I would say, are best delivered with a smile.

My formula, accordingly, has always been systems *and* smiles.

Not too many companies are good at both. A few years back, my family was planning to move just a few miles and a local moving company was recommended to us. The movers' smiles were as broad as the day is long—I assume that's why the company got those recommendations.

Somehow in the sea of smiles, I missed a fact about its operating procedure: Our dozens of boxes had approximate names scrawled on them like "girl's bedroom," "his office," etc. But there was no numbering system, no real tagging system. In other words: no way to prove if every box had made the move. Or hadn't.

This situation seemed all right (again, the smiles went a long way—too far, I guess, in a sense), until we found ourselves missing something, a small work of art we'd bought years ago, precious to us for nostalgic reasons.

Could the sweet little local moving company help us? Uh, no. There was no way to trace where, or when, or even *if* a box had gone missing. There were no smiles anywhere once this reality sunk in.

> Systems and smiles—the two will take you a long way. More than twice as far as one or the other.

# pour lion and pepi

Autonomy and standards aren't necessarily opposing forces. At the old Ritz-Carlton, the lion lovingly etched in the side of each wine glass served two purposes: (1) the lion promoted the brand and (2) the tiny, engraved *tongue* of the lion served as the pour line, helping to ensure that the appropriate amount of wine was served. Ask Ritz-Carlton employees of that era, and they'll still point with pride and a sort of insider's knowingness to this subtly reinforced standard.

Why did the Ritz-Carlton's employees take pride in something that actually *reduced* their autonomy? First, because protecting Ritz-Carlton assets (in this case, wine) was a stated company value (see Chapter 5). And variations—inevitable when you don't have a pour line—are one of five key defects tracked in the Toyota-inspired Ritz view of the world. A companywide understanding of this as a goal, taught at The Ritz-Carlton through the acronym "Mr. Biv" (avoiding *M*istakes, *R*eworks, *B*reakdowns, *I*nefficiencies, and *V*ariations in work proc esses), makes all the difference in instilling the value of a standard among people who otherwise value autonomy. In addition, the elegant etched-lion implementation of the standard, on the "tip of the tongue," so to speak, let employees uphold the standard without appearing slavish.

In more life-and-death situations, you would think that just hammering in the standards would work: "Don't mix up the Heparin doses—OR ELSE!" Unfortunately, barring Colonial Williamsburg–style stocks being moved onsite, this works less completely than one would expect.

What *does* work when you need to enforce standards? Consider my acronym PEPI (pronounced "peppy"):

**Purpose:** Employees have a clear sense of purpose—and how the standard fits into it.

**Enforce intelligently**: Keep things visual, train, and reinforce.

**Peer pressure**: Positive peer pressure is a must.

**Input:** Employees are able to have a say in the refinements, changes, and even possible future abolition of the standard.

## conveying standards—and maintaining autonomy

What's the secret of conveying standards? Most of all, you need to set your people up to succeed, with the patience and good steering that keeps everyone working toward the same goal. Let me close this chapter with a story that illustrates the adaptability and steady hand that can be required for conveying standards successfully.

Isadore Sharp tells the story of training staff in service standards and how this can be accomplished even when the staff themselves, drawn from the local population and chosen for traits rather than for prior experience, have never experienced such service. Sharp himself only realized how much patience and understanding this can require after he visited an under-resourced island where his company, Four Seasons, had recently built a resort.

> I ordered room service. A young lady came in with my order and set it up on the terrace. "Where did you learn to do this?" I asked her. "What job did you have before?"
>
> "Oh, I never worked before," she told me. "This was my first job, sir."
>
> "Then how did you learn to do this? There are a lot of items, and everything's here, placed exactly as it should be."
>
> "Well, sir, they taught me everything."
>
> "That's interesting," I said. "How did they do that?"
>
> "They let me take everything home for me to practice with my family," she explained.

I began to realize what John [Strauss, the manager in charge of training at this resort] had meant by patience and understanding. He had put in place a training program for people with absolutely no conception of international hotel service; let alone how to achieve it. He had done this through judging, by attitude, whom we should or shouldn't hire, then patiently helping them understand how and why we did things, and doing this in a way that wouldn't make them reluctant to go on asking questions until they got it right.[9]

While allowing employees to take work home with them may not be what's called for in your situation, creating an environment where asking questions and making mistakes is absolutely encouraged and support is provided by peers, may be exactly what you *are* looking for.

## "and your point is?"

▸ Your employees need to understand their purpose in your organization and be given the power and encouragement to act autonomously to support that purpose, or you'll lose customers from your lack of flexibility. Employees hired, oriented, and reinforced properly, surrounded by peers of the same caliber, will thrive when given significant autonomy—and wither otherwise.

▸ All pay being approximately equal, an employee will sprint to the employer that offers more freedom.

▸ You *want* customer relations to be on the shoulders of your employees. But as long as you're defining every little thing—and rewarding/punishing based on seemingly arbitrary criteria—you won't get them to carry that responsibility.

▸ The orientation period is when you can make great strides toward getting the most out of your team. This orientation should be led by the highest possible level in the company (ideally, the CEO) and stress the purpose of every employee, while making it clear an employee will be *celebrated* for rising to her purpose in the organization. (And won't be scolded, for example, for being a few short in the number of linens changed because she stopped to help a customer in need.)

➤ Standards help ensure that every part of your service reflects the best way your company knows how to perform it, a prescription that is then modified to the best of the ability of your autonomously performing employee to suit the needs and wishes, expressed or unexpressed, of the actual customer the employee's facing. The summary statement for a standard should include the following:

- Why the service is of *value* (why we're doing this in the first place)

- The *emotional response* we're aiming to have the customer feel

- The expected *way* to accomplish the service

➤ When you need to enforce standards, consider my acronym PEPI (pronounced "peppy"):

**P**urpose

**E**nforce intelligently

**P**eer pressure

**I**nput

➤ Training for standards requires patience and flexibility: setting your employees up to succeed.

part three

# the rise of self-service and social media—and other seismic shifts

# chapter 8

# the rise of self-service

## a boon to your customers—but only if you do it right

employees aren't the only ones with an expanded inclination toward autonomy. Today's *customers* also have an increasing desire for—and expectation of—autonomy, in the form of self-service options. This is a very powerful trend among today's customers, with some customers wanting to do business with you *wholly* in a self-service environment and even more now growing accustomed to augmenting human service providers with self-service . . . as I myself did not long ago with my smartphone when shopping at the local music store.

## awarding myself the mobile prize

One Saturday morning, I found myself trekking to the guitar store uptown because I needed strings for a "Baby Taylor." (A Baby Taylor is a reduced-sized version of a standard acoustic guitar.) The clerk, who was knowledgeable in an approximate sort of way, told me he thought medium-gauge, full-length guitar strings would work well: just cut off the excess length as needed to make them fit the "baby." I had a hunch that his answer might be incomplete, and I vaguely wondered why the clerk didn't look in his system for Taylor's "manufacturer's stringing recommendation" before advising me. I didn't wonder for long, though, before turning the issue over to my iPhone. With just a few thumb strokes—"What kind of strings should I use on my Baby Taylor?"—I found an official, enthusiastically detailed description of which strings to use and why the decision matters:

> [Here at Taylor,] we install light-gauge Elixir NANOWEB strings (.012 on high E) on Baby Taylors. We recommend you stick with lights when you replace them . . . our ever-vigilant repair guys, who are the ultimate judges of what works and doesn't work on our guitars . . . [say that] using anything but light-gauge strings puts too much . . . "pull" on a Baby, [and] the intonation and one's ability to keep them in tune become problematic.[1]

Thus, by using self-service to address my situation as a customer, a very particular situation (probably only one out of hundreds of guitars that come into that store each year is a Baby Taylor), I found the precise answer that potentially saved my guitar from never sounding quite right. In many service situations, it's inevitable that the customer knows key information himself, *feels* he knows it himself, or has more time to invest in addressing his own situation than the human service provider does. This is one of the appeals of modern self-service.

Apple Stores have recognized this race-to-the-gadgets phenomenon and addressed it by putting specially programmed iPad stations (dubbed "Smart Signs") beside its products so customers will stay and gadgetsource their questions in an Apple-centered system rather than have the customers leave the Apple system or the physical premises, either of which could lead to customers getting distracted from the Apple gospel. On these iPad Smart Signs you can, for example, explore features and compare a variety of models of laptops, or figure out how much a new phone will *really* cost you, based on your personal carrier and rate plan. And when you're ready for human help, you can page an employee directly from the iPad.

Royal Caribbean Cruises has responded somewhat similarly, even though, unlike the case at Apple, its passengers assuredly *cannot* leave without significant watery consequences. The latest Royal Caribbean ship, *Allure of the Seas*, is built with touch-screen kiosks on every deck acting as self-service concierges, offering "what to do right now" and "room finder" information.[2]

### Self-Service: From Sketchy Backwater to the Mainstream of Customer Service

Richard Carlile, a British publisher, bookseller, and campaigner for press and voting rights, spent 1819 until 1823 in prison for distributing the banned works of radicals and reformists and exposés of officially sanctioned massacres.

As soon as he was sprung from prison, Carlile tried to skirt the law and prevent his reincarceration by creating the world's first version of Redbox-for-books: a machine that "dropped a customer's desired book after money was inserted and a dial positioned to a corresponding number," thus not technically involving Carlile in the selling (or so he argued to the court when he was re-arrested).[3]

For nearly two centuries following, as Christopher D. Salyers notes in his book *Vending Machines: Coined Consumerism*, self-service similarly seemed a bit like getting away with something: snacks with more salt than the doctor recommended, condoms, hangover remedies, cigarettes for minors who have exact change, or in certain machines in Japan even more sketchy products—all dispensed away from the eyes of onlookers.[4]

It's tempting to think the secretive era of self-service is emphatically over: Out in the open, using airline kiosks or shopping online from their mobile phones, self-service is right smack in the mainstream of what today's customers expect from the service experience. But we should also remember that the impulse to privacy, to isolation really, is alive and well and driving many self-service interactions (or should I call them anti-interactions?).

Some customers are inherently, or temporarily, ill at ease with other human beings—gun-shy from previous encounters with surly desk clerks, hung over, or, most likely late at night, bombed out of their minds. But they still want to do business with you, and, by and large, you still want them to. Remembering that the trend toward self-service indeed owes some of its momentum to these quirky human factors is an important, if odd, reality to keep in mind when designing and refining it.

In a *business-to-business* context as well, self-service can make itself valuable by incorporating details that only the customer knows, or knows best. In the follow-up to a keynote speech I gave to The Payroll Group, an independent trade association, I was struck recently by the extent to which these payroll service providers have moved to a model where clients themselves, through remote software, enter and verify small details like the precise spellings of their employees' names, leading to reduced errors.

Companies today have a choice:

- ▶ Embrace the modern inclination to self-service

- ▶ Ignore it

- ▶ Chafe at it

- ▶ Get overly aggressive and force it down the throats of all their customers

The name of the game is to embrace self-service as a way to provide *anticipatory* service. Happily, self-service is likely to be anticipatory *by its nature,* due to its ability to accept unique, customized input from the customers themselves, and smart self-service design can further enhance this. Truly great self-service is anticipatory in that it helps suggest choices and behaviors in an intelligent manner: IBM's technology in dressing rooms that suggests complementary ties based on the sportswear you're trying on; airport kiosk messaging that protects you with a warning to take *both* of your documents—receipt and boarding pass—based on the experience of previous passengers who were stranded at the gate lacking what they needed to board; suggestions from online merchants for additional items to add to your order, based on what you *really* would benefit from—suggestions that are crowdsourced or expertly curated, but in any event not based on an online equivalent of racking up fees.

# principles of successful self-service

Self-service follows specific, predictable rules.

1. **Customers need a choice of channels.** A choice means they choose, and you respect their decisions. Customers shouldn't be calling you on the phone only to have you tell them, "You should go to the website." (Incredibly, this happens all the time.) There's a *reason* they called you on the phone, so talk to them! (Note that this isn't mutually exclusive with the possibility that the call may be because your website is broken/limited/poorly designed, thus necessitating a "stupid-stuff" call the customer didn't want to make. See Chapter 10.)

For example, there's a hotel chain that continuously—and I mean, continuously— urges me to use automated kiosk check-in. They send me emails at spaced intervals every time I'm about to visit one of their properties, urging me to use their new machines. I ignore the emails, arrive at the hotel, go to the front desk, and am told, "You know, you didn't have to come up here. You could have used the kiosk." But I *want* to be checked in by a human. It's a central part of the hospitality experience for me. And the choice should be mine.

2. **Self-service needs to have escape hatches**. Here are a couple of examples:

> ► Automated confirmation letters need to come from, or at least prominently feature, a reply-to address. When huge companies send confirmations that end with "Please do not reply," it's a kiss-off. When smaller companies do this, they just look ridiculous. Either way, it can lead customers to desperation. The asymmetry defies our human desire for reciprocity: The company is sending you a letter, but prohibiting you from writing back!

► When you end your FAQs and similar self-help postings with "Did this answer your question?" contemplate what should happen if the customer's response is "No, it didn't answer my question." First, consider what this customer response means: The customer has *tried* to do your company's work for you—honestly tried—and failed, which means *you* have failed. Here's what should follow: An "I'm so sorry; we obviously have room for improvement. Click here and a live human being will assist you." Or "If you would like a phone call from a human, please enter your number here. When we call, our humans will have a complete record of your query/issue and its failed resolution, and we will make it right."

3. **Don't make your customers think about your organizational chart.** *Customers don't care about the structure of your company; they don't want to learn how your company is organized.* This is a really, really big one. Think of a master self-service merchandiser like Amazon.com. Yeah, it still has some hierarchical menus on its site, but as the site has evolved, those menus have diminished in importance to the point that they're nearly unnoticeable. What has replaced them?

► **An incredibly effective "Customers who viewed this item also viewed" field,** with images and names of the most popular items that have been considered for purchase by other customers Amazon.com thinks are similar to you.

► **A big honkin' search field** that works well to find just about anything you need, using the terms in which *you* think. (And if you don't find what you're looking for using the terms you entered, there's a "give feedback about your search" button at the bottom of the search.)

► **Absolutely zero use of Amazon.com's internal terminology,** nor any need to think in terms of "returns departments," "credits," "technical support," "account services," etc. Amazon.com is a unique company with its own internal jargon, yet none of that leaks into what the customer encounters; everything is in normal English.

4. **Usability is a science that needs to be respected**. Reinventing the wheel as far as usability is self-defeating: Usability is a well-tested science, yet people keep trying to wing it. For example, why do people hate—truly love to hate—IVRs (telephone interactive voice response)? In part, because so many companies ignore or try end runs around the rules of usability for such systems. For example, most humans can't retain in memory more than thirty seconds of information at a time, so an IVR with more than thirty seconds of options or information is just going to confuse customers. There are similar hard-and-fast rules about how many menu items a customer can remember, yet some companies mangle their application of this rule by loading up each option with suboptions: "For Office A, Office B, or Office C, press 1." That one single suboption actually demands that the customer remember four things: three departments and the menu number.[5] In addition to the limits of human memory, there are conventions to adhere to in order to keep your customers comfortable: For example, "0" on a telephone menu should take you to a human, and the search bar on a web page should be exactly where customers expect it: right at the top of the page.

5. **Customers need to be able to shift lanes.** No matter what channel your customer enters through—your website, a phone line, email, etc.—it should be a seamless and cohesive process. It shouldn't feel like an entirely different experience in each area, and it shouldn't make customers start from scratch if they've already shared information with your company through another channel.

## Channel Surfing

Remember that customers may use different channels in different ways. Some customers buy only on the web but like to *visit* brick-and-mortar stores as a tactile experience. (Note: In the case of a grocery store, this balance may lean in the exact opposite direction.) They may, say, visit the Orvis store once a year, but always place their Orvis orders online. If your physical stores are thus taking on the role of a sampling location where a customer touches and feels products for later purchases on your website, it's not necessarily a negative for your brand, if handled appropriately. However, it does need to be planned for. It can be sabotaged quickly, for example, by an overly aggressive commission structure, or it can be enhanced by discount or QR codes (QR codes are those two-dimensional bar-codes that take you, via scanner, directly to a specific website) that let web or mobile purchases track back to store visits.

6. **Self-service can't be set and then forgotten. It's an endless work in progress.** It's not like those ads you see in the back of entre-preneurial magazines that promise an easy living owning vending machines: Set them up, ignore them, come back once in a while to check on them like a trap you set in the woods, and see all the money you've caught. Modern self-service isn't like that. It has to be moni-tored and reviewed regularly. Specifically, every time you set up a proc-ess, you need to set up a monitoring plan for it.

For example, at my company, Oasis, I set up an automated, instant confirmation greeting for people who have requested our catalog online. This greeting goes out, via auto-response email, to welcome prospective customers and invite them to start making use of the links on our website right away, without having to wait the few days it takes for the physical catalog to slither its way to them via the U.S. mail. To be friendly, I include all the names of our client advisers, since at this point a particular adviser hasn't been assigned. The problem? Well, even though we have low staff turnover, occasionally people leave or change positions. So, if this letter stays static, eventually someone is going to get a letter with names of *former* client advisers. Other information and links in the letter may change eventually as well. So I set up a process that ensures I myself receive the confirmation letter at regular intervals so I can review it. Simple solution.

If you don't set up procedures like this, you end up looking like the hotel whose setup I was asked to review not long ago. In each hotel room there was a laminated card that read, "Two steps to get online! Find the internet cable that's in the desk drawer, and open up your browser!" Unfortunately, there not only was no cable in the drawer, there was no Ethernet jack anywhere in the room. The service had apparently been changed to Wi-Fi, which would've been fine if only the documentation had come along for the ride.

7. **Your staff needs to have used—recently—your self-service channels.** Otherwise they won't ever recommend, understand the issues with, or be able to converse intelligently with a customer about using them.

8. **Ugly upsells through self-service are a brand killer.** The way Amazon.com handles upselling is ideal: "Frequently bought with" messaging gently tells you what customers who are similar to you also purchased (and lost sales are avoided by "customers who viewed this product ended up buying _____" in case the first product page you land on doesn't prove a perfect fit). Harder sells are especially hazardous in self-service, as there's no human tone of voice. If you do want to try a more direct upsell, I would suggest some kind of tongue-in-cheek humor to tone it down. Recognize the obviously awkward nature of the electronic relationship and use a humorous acknowledgment of this to modulate it.

◆ ◆ ◆ ◆ ◆

Self-service isn't just the wave of the future; it's the reality of the present. Embrace it—your customers already have.

# "and your point is?"

► The name of the game is using self-service to provide *anticipatory* service.

► Great self-service is anticipatory because it helps suggest choices and behaviors in an intelligent manner to customers, often via details volunteered by the customer herself.

▸ Customers need a choice of channels. A choice means they *choose*, and you *respect*, their decisions.

▸ Self-service needs to come with escape hatches. For example, automated confirmation letters need to come from, or at least prominently feature, an address you can reply to. When you add "Did this answer your question?" in FAQs and similar self-help postings, think through what should happen if the customer's response is "No!"

▸ Everything should be organized and described from a customer's perspective. Customers don't care about the structure of your business; they don't want to have to understand how it's organized.

▸ When developing self-help tools and processes, remember that usability is a science.

▸ Customers need to be able to shift channels no matter how they initially enter your company (via email, online, in-store, etc.), without it being jarring.

▸ Remember that customers may use different channels in different ways. If handled appropriately and planned for, this doesn't have to be a negative for your brand.

▸ Self-service can't be set and then forgotten. It's an endless work in progress, and processes are required to regularly monitor it.

▸ Your staff members need to have used your self-service channels; otherwise they won't be able to converse intelligently with a customer about using them.

▸ Ugly upsells through self-service are a brand killer; subtlety is key.

# chapter 9

# technological change and disabled customers

## a true opportunity, if you avoid the missteps

serving—anticipating—the needs and wishes of people with disabilities is a true opportunity. I know that sounds like clichéd happy-talk, but I mean it: People with disabilities constitute a large and growing segment of the populace, a factor that should be enough to encourage you to commit, with a sincere smile rather than a grudging grimace, to serving them. Furthermore, the public whom you serve includes an even larger, and also growing, proportion of people who are children of, parents of, spouses of, siblings of, or simply fond of people with disabilities. So don't assume that showing active kindness to this segment will go unrewarded or, on the negative side of the ledger, that callousness will go unnoticed.

## there's more to ramping up than putting ramps up: a variety of issues and solutions

People in our society with disabilities include those who use wheelchairs, and many who don't. (In fact, the universal use of the wheelchair symbol to indicate disability may be responsible for some confusion on this front.) The spectrum includes visual disabilities of greater and lesser severity, chronic pain, lack of manual dexterity, and other issues that are less visible yet affect our customers and their loved ones.

For people with disabilities, technology is a double-edged sword. In obvious ways, technology can be a godsend: from automobiles and mass transit to (some) e-readers, from medical advances to assistive-technology devices controllable by body gestures, technology has the ability to make life better for people with disabilities, now and in the future. The other edge of the sword cuts in when technology is advanced without consideration for how people with disabilities are using the current iteration of the technology. This has happened repeatedly—and with stunning speed—as internet commerce and mobile technology have advanced.

Be sensitive to this when providing customer care. Not all your customers *can* interact with your IVR (interactive voice response telephone systems)—they may have hearing loss or vocal limitations to the point that it's not possible—making it important that you offer an alternative. Not everyone can see the graphics-intensive website you're so proud of—it may be entirely unreadable by blind customers who depend on screen-reading technology. This is why it's so important that you follow good accessibility protocols in designing your website. (If your web designer says, "What's that?" or "That's not important" when you bring up accessibility, take your business elsewhere or partner your web designer with an expert in this area.)

Mobile technology can be especially problematic, in part because of the miniaturization inherent in this field and in part because changes in the field have been so rapid. Here, even an overwhelmingly positive case in point brings up some issues: The iPhone is one of the most encouraging examples in this regard, packed with accessible technologies, including type you can zoom to many times its original size to compensate for moderate visual impairments, built-in TTY compatibility for the deaf (TTY, also known as TDD, is a two-ended system that allows someone with hearing or speech limitations to communicate on the phone using a keyboard), and more. Not to mention Siri—the extraordinary voice-based personal assistant. [Disclosure: Nuance, and its acquired brand MacSpeech, where I've been a long-time investor, is involved in the current generation of speech recognition technology.] And Apple has been excellent at holding third-party vendors to accessibility standards if they want their software on the iPhone. Yet the fact remains that this largely accessible marvel of technology comes in a nearly flat device, almost entirely lacking in the traditional grasping points and tactile cues of a standard telephone and keypad, making it hard to handle or even hold for people with certainly physical limitations. This being one of the most *positive* examples, imagine how paradoxical other evolving technology can be for those with disabilities.

Netflix, while well known for providing excellent customer support over the telephone, has caused a problem for the Deaf community by *entirely eliminating the option to contact the company by email.* What could be more welcome for someone who can't hear than to use email to reach customer service or tech support? Well, the ability to use plain old email or chat, or anything other than voice to contact Netflix is exactly what the Deaf community asked for . . . in 2007. Read a deaf customer's comments below, along with Netflix's response. (Netflix in bold italic, customer in regular type.)

Netflix:     ***Earlier this week someone posted this to the blog comments:***

Customer:   I am BEYOND frustrated with your website.
            I can find NO WAY to contact customer service except via telephone!!!
            There is no email anywhere under CONTACT US.

            There is no online "chat" type of service either.
            Have you never thought you might have a HEARING IMPAIRED customer that cannot use a PHONE? [. . .]

Netflix:     ***This was an excellent question, and today I received this note from the Customer Service*** *team: I am completing training of our agents today for the TTY system . . . I have tested the line through a TTY service, and the line is functional. The number that will be used for TTY Customer Service is 1-866-402-2619.*

Nice . . . until you try this number (I have): It doesn't work, even though Netflix continues to post it as the TTY alternative on its contact pages, for example, http://ir.netflix.com/contactus.cfm.[1]

Don't make the same mistake yourself. My point *isn't* that you necessarily have to offer TTY or other fancy assistive technology when you're running an online commerce site, as long as you're careful not to block the disabled at the gates through faulty communication policies and processes: For instance, don't eliminate support by email (à la Netflix) and don't use heavy graphics on your website without making allowances for accessibility. These and other thoughtless actions will leave you dead in the water with certain disabled populations.

Another lesson you would do well to learn, which, again, Netflix doesn't seem to understand, is that technology and processes that benefit people with disabilities often benefit the rest of us as well: for example, clearly labeled website elements, "universal design" in buildings (such as those easy-to-use lever-style door "knobs" even the able-bodied appreciate when loaded down with groceries), and closed captioning (subtitles), against which Netflix has been running a highly publicized battle, initially refusing and then dragging its feet on implementation of subtitles for its streamed videos. Captioning clearly benefits the fully deaf and the moderately hard of hearing, as well as fully abled people in noisy environments and movie buffs who want to catch the intricacies of dialog. An overall win, one would think, but in its shortsighted opposition, Netflix has brought forces together against it, including cultural icons like Marlee Matlin, in a battle that makes little sense.

Efforts to block the enemies of technology—spammers and hackers—can also end up barring the disabled, in this case those with visual impairments. Websites try to protect themselves from spammers and hackers by requiring the input of a CAPTCHA (CAPTCHA is a laborious acronym for Completely Automated Public Turing test to tell Computers and Humans Apart) to join a site or use its contact forms. But by doing so without an audio alternative or other nonvisual substitute is to lock out customers who have sight impairments. This is bad business, unethical, and potentially illegal, by violating Section 508.[2] (Section 508, an amendment to the United States Workforce Rehabilitation Act of 1973, is the federal law requiring that all electronic and information technology developed, procured, maintained, or used by the federal government be accessible to people with disabilities—further defining "accessibility" as the ability to be used as effectively by those with disabilities as by those without.[3]) Note, though, that many of the available audio alternatives to CAPTCHAs are incredibly difficult to use as well (try one out yourself and see what I mean!), so be thoughtful in choosing and implementing these, too.

## wynn some

I'm going to end here with a little technological silver lining: the use of, if not high-tech, at least *mezzo* tech by Wynn Resorts to assist the disabled. When visiting Vegas to give a speech to a hospitality organization on a beautiful June day, I saw a huge ceramic trash can at the front entrance of The Wynn that seemed to be blocking the push switch for disabled access. However, on closer inspection, I saw the disabled-access switch was apparently motion activated, with an indication on it reading "Wave to open." Curious, I gave a little wave of my hand from where I was standing—*eight feet away*. The technology worked like magic: no need to struggle to move the clearly unmovable trash can, no need to wonder if a clunky old mechanical push button was broken (as they often are), no need to exert the arm strength sometimes unreasonably asked of those in wheelchairs.

I'm not sure whether this extra technological courtesy is thanks to Steve Wynn's sensibilities concerning disabilities or is a sign of the overall advanced thinking of his hotel development team, but either way I want to say: Nice going. Technology, combined with thoughtfulness, can go a long way. (Visit www.micahsolomon.com to see photos of this Wynn entrance.)

# "and your point is?"

- ▶ People with disabilities constitute a large and growing segment of the populace. And the public we serve includes an even larger proportion of people who are related to, responsible for, or simply fond of people with disabilities. Therefore, showing active kindness to this segment isn't something to assume will go unrewarded, and showing callousness isn't something to assume will go unnoticed.

- ▶ Problems arise when technology advances without consideration for how people with disabilities are using current technology.

- ▶ It's important that you follow good accessibility protocols in designing your website; remember, not everyone can see it as you do, and similarly remember that audio-based technology like IVRs (interactive voice response telephony systems) may not work for those with hearing impairments.

- ▶ Websites try to protect themselves from spammers and hackers by requiring the input of a CAPTCHA, but doing so without an audio alternative—a *good* audio alternative—is to exclude customers with visual impairments.

- ▶ Technology that's necessary for people with disabilities also often makes life easier for the able-bodied.

# chapter 10

# shoulder your customer's burden (and make sure you're not adding to it!)

taking on customer burdens as your own, and taking care to eliminate anything you may be *adding* to that burden (wasting their time, tripping them up with inaccurate or incomplete information, taxing customer patience and memory with poorly designed systems), is central to modern, anticipatory, technologically informed service.

The most pervasive way businesses add to the burden on their customers is by *wasting their time*. I recommend tackling this issue for starters; it sounds mundane, but a lot of creativity can go into attacking this problem with gusto. Your business should be a fumble-free zone where you actively avoid wasting the time of customers, especially time wasted in *repeated* efforts by customers on inanities that can be better handled by improving your company's processes.

## stupid stuff

Here's a paradox: If you're going to successfully bind customers to you and build lasting customer loyalty, it helps to have touch points: chances to interact. *But these touch points shouldn't be occurring because of broken processes.* For example, the questions customers are forced to call you with after they've searched for the answers to those same questions on your website or your mobile app—and found them nowhere. Or phone calls because your product keeps breaking on them in the exact same way, but word isn't getting to your engineering team to get the update out that will fix it. These impositions on your customers are what I call "stupid stuff" (although depending on the squeamishness of the client and the absurdity of the context, "stuff" might or might not be the actual "*s* word" I use). Bill Price and David Jaffe, in their refreshing manifesto *The Best Service Is No Service*, similarly call these moments "dumb contacts."[1]

Take a twofold attitude, companywide, when a customer calls. On the one hand, be delighted that she called. A call from a customer, truly, is an opportunity. Marketing departments spend dozens, sometimes hundreds, of dollars of promotion to make the phone ring a single time. So to have a live customer on the phone is, indeed, something to be valued. On the other hand, realize that the customer may not actually *want* to be calling. And that too many forced calls for "stupid stuff" will ultimately drive your customers away. It follows logically, then, that every customer service call deserves to be analyzed. Why did the call come in? Was it for a customer-driven reason or a broken-process reason? I'm fond of Zappos CEO Tony Hsieh's theory that people call his company for all sorts of reasons: It's late at night and they feel a bit lonely; it feels odd for them to order shoes on the web without *ever* having talked to someone at the company; or even because they want to test if Zappos customer service is really as good as it claims to be.[2] All of these are legitimate, customer-driven reasons. But I'm concerned about the host of calls that come in because of a burden you've placed on the customer. *These* are the reasons that will drive away your customers.

## stupid is as . . . i forget

To analyze calls for stupid stuff requires a deft touch. Thanks to misuse of CRM (customer relationship management) software, the vast majority of companies tend to have far too *many* codes for call sources, sometimes numbering into the thousands, while other companies throw up their hands and drop everything into catchalls that are completely meaningless, such as "returns" or "shipping." Amazon.com had three hundred and sixty codes to choose from at one point—three hundred for email and sixty for telephone contacts—before reforming its ways, says Bill Price, Amazon.com's first vice president of global customer service. Its lesson is an excellent one for all of us.

> Amazon once had 360 customer contact codes . . . some created at the behest of a "store" marketing manager, IT, or the legal department. The company frequently added or removed codes, requiring ongoing training for the agents and even a metric to track "code use compliance." Few of these early codes attached to an owner [in other words, became the specific responsibility of a high-level Amazon.com manager], and the company fell into the trap of presenting weekly "top ten" codes, which rarely moved up or down one position, and which, by design, ignored the 350 reasons looming in the darkness below the top ten. The company decided to reengineer the contact coding system, . . . resulting in thirty codes that could be entered directly into the CRM system, each with an owner in the MECE tradition [MECE is the McKinsey & Co. acronym for mutually exclusive and collectively exhaustive], codes that would never change . . . and they haven't, after all these years.[3]

Some reasons for calls are deep-seated. Resolving these issues is more likely with the system suggested above: that codes should each have an owner at the company, and *only one* owner. Once you identify an owner, via calls sourced to him that appear to represent incoming "stupid stuff," you can get down to work—involving your vendors, your engineers, everyone needed to eliminate the source of the call.

Now if some of these call codes show repeat calls from the same customer (and some of them will) you need to figure out what this means. Poor training or poor technology? Either of these can be systematically addressed, once you identify it as the problem. Or the repeat calls may mean that you're rushing customers off the phone because of misguided metrics that encourage short calls—a mistake so common it should be one of the first places you look: In my experience, limiting time per call is one of the top causes of repeat calls. Not having enough time to solve a customer problem is also one of the top causes of call center burnout. It's a prime way to create what psychologist Martin Seligman famously termed "learned helplessness" among good employees who really do wish they were able to assist customers thoroughly, rather than rushing them off the phone with an incomplete solution.[4] Breeding helplessness in employees is dangerous. It's the utter, absolute opposite of optimism, the "O" in WETCO.

Odds are good that the codes, correctly tracked, are going to show a variety of causes, from simple, predictable queries such as (for a bank or credit union) "when is my mortgage due?" to more complex and sometimes truly unique issues. Coming close to eliminating the more predictable queries is something you can do if, like Amazon.com CEO Jeff Bezos, you commit to inventing on behalf of your customers. By inventing, Bezos doesn't only mean huge strides like his Kindle e-reader that has transformed the publishing and reading landscape. He's also talking about eliminating stupid stuff. Amazon.com, Schwab.com, and other savvy organizations frequently invent ahead of their customers by tracking the stupid-stuff calls and eliminating them through proactively delivered confirmations and other creative methods, leaving staff free to handle the more complex and unusual issues that crop up.

Just because customers haven't *asked* you to eliminate stupid stuff for them doesn't mean they don't want you to. I remember the days when you didn't know whether Amazon.com had received your order and you had to try to call to find out. (That's right: *call.*) Then, one day, order confirmations started to arrive every time you placed an order— first within a few minutes, now within what seems like a few milliseconds. By anticipating their customers' desire to not be on the phone talking about stupid stuff, Bezos and team became very profitable pioneers.

### This Book Won't Help You . . . If the Stupid-Stuff Calls You Get Are *Intentional*

We bought a house recently, complete with what seemed to be a functioning furnace. The furnace had been built by a major HVAC manufacturer that had carefully cultivated a premium reputation, a reputation that dissolved quickly for us once we moved in. Immediately, the furnace quit, requiring a $1,600 repair. That's okay, I thought: The previous homeowners had sprung for an extended warranty, which, being organized people, they had the Realtor turn over to us in a folder of household documents at closing. So, trying to schedule a warranty repair, I called the perfectly nice people at the company that had *installed* the furnace, but the exchange unfortunately went as follows:

**Furnace Installers:** "Oh, you must be the Jacobsens."

**Micah:** "No, we're the people who bought the Jacobsens' house."

**Furnace Installers:** "Sorry, we can't help you. The manufacturer requires you to have the Jacobsens transfer the warranty. But it only costs $25. You'll need to print out a verification form from the internet, have the Jacobsens both sign it, and mail it to the manufacturer in [home state of manufacturer], and a week or two later you'll get a new warranty certificate."

**Micah:** "But we've never even *met* the Jacobsens and my understanding is they now live across the country. We don't know how to reach them very easily, and our furnace is out *now*."

**Furnace Installers:** "I'm sorry."

To my mind, the manufacturer wasn't looking to get our $25 warranty transfer fee. *Its goal was to keep us from using the warranty*, so the manufacturer could avoid the entire $1,600 repair cost. I mean, seriously: This unit weighs *tons*. It's not going anywhere; there's no switcheroo possible. Which means the calls I was forced to make to track down the Jacobsens (who, against all odds and against the HVAC manufacturer's expectations, did transfer the warranty to us), as well as my later hounding of the furnace manufacturer to get them to honor the warranty, were all *intentionally created* stupid-stuff calls.

Are draconian customer policies full of intentional gotchas, sneaky expiration dates, and hidden fees the reasons for *your* stupid-stuff phone calls? If so, this book isn't going to help your company. Customers may have accepted this anti-consumer behavior pre-Twitter, pre-Facebook. But in the age of social media, the balance of power has changed.

## get to them first

Beyond not wasting their time, it's time to have a policy and mindset of using communications technology and automation to let customers hear from you *before they have to ask for anything themselves*.

Like much else in customer service, this requires a masterful touch, far removed from the hamfistedness of a spammer. Applied properly, the principle of "getting to them first" is a powerful way to make customers feel remembered, cared for, and, ultimately and paradoxically, left alone and unbothered, since they can now relax knowing you will, for example:

▶ Notify passengers if flights have been delayed or gates change, and if the worst happens (a cancellation) rebook them and alert them to the new arrangements, without any work on the passengers' part.

▶ Reach out to customers if there's a delay in shipping the item you'd promised to deliver before the holidays.

▶ Remind customers of something they "should" be keeping track of themselves, but that you, in your quest to become their irreplaceable vendor, are happy to put on your own shoulders. For example, you can remind them, before they ask, when their mortgage payments are due or when a medication needs to be refilled.

Along these lines, my credit card company has cozied up to me by taking what should be my responsibility—posting my payments on time—off my shoulders and put it on the company's. Now, as a result, I'm rarely late on my credit card payments these days, and I don't really think of switching companies anymore, thanks to the simple automated alert sent to my inbox:

> *Alert: Your Payment Is Due in 10 Days to X Card Services*
> To: micah@micahsolomon.com
> Your payment to us will be due in 10 days, for your account that ends in 1111.

This sense of being able to relax in a company's electronically anticipatory arms is analogous to the sense of being cared for in a childhood home, the archetype we're using for ideal customer service. This effect is enhanced by making sure that every automated addition to your repertoire is accompanied by an option for the recipient to easily reach a human being. Remember, your marketing department *would spill its blood* to reach a live customer one on one; this isn't an overhead expense. It's an opportunity So strive to offer customers a chance to talk with a human, if that's their preference, even when you're reaching out to them through automation.

# where are the opportunities to get to them first?

Here are the opportunities you'll find to get to your customers first:

▶ **With anything you think about more than/more frequently than your customers do.** If your business is a mail-order pharmacy, it means you work all day on the intricacies of injectable medications. These are expensive and involved medications used for managing multiple sclerosis and other chronic illnesses, requiring pre-approvals from insurance agencies, typically shipped to the customer every ninety days. Your customer, on the other hand, has a life. She's doing everything *other than* thinking about her medication supply in the eighty-nine-day span between reorders. So, you set up the ultimate in bulletproof reminder systems, check for her that insurance and physician verifications have remained up to date, etc., and handle everything for her as transparently as possible, thus becoming her indispensable dispensary.

▶ **Any time your customers would otherwise be waiting in the dark.** Projects and products built or shipped in stages, from insurance applications and disaster relief efforts to cross-country relocations and event planning, are important opportunities to get to your customers first. "No news is good news" isn't something customers assume or should assume. Regular updates should be your mode of operation.

▶ **With anything that customers need to know about, if you're aware of it before they are.** This could be protection from a new software virus; many stitches are saved when electronic patches are provided to customers *before* they need them. Or, let's look at an application from the fine-arts world: Don't make your patrons find out for themselves that a sporting event has closed off the normal route to the ballet. Sure, they've already bought their nonrefundable tickets *this* time, but they may never buy them again or become that legacy donor you've been looking for if they encounter an aggravating experience that leaves a poor taste in their mouths. So I was impressed one evening when, courteously and cannily, the ticketing service used by the Philadelphia Ballet sent an automated call to my phone to alert me to leave extra time so as not to miss the opening curtain that Saturday—which we would have by at least forty-five minutes. It also coupled the phone call—just for safety—with an email, as follows:

> An important message regarding your performance on Saturday at 12 p.m. The International Dragon Boat Festival and the U.S. Pro Bike Race will take place Saturday. Throughout the day Kelly Drive will be partially closed and MLK Drive will be completely closed. Please allow extra time to arrive at the Academy of Music for your 12 p.m. performance.

## I'm from the Government—And I'm Here to Save Your Life

Some government agencies and regulated utilities have learned the importance of getting to customers first better than their counterparts have in the private sector. Consider our power company in the Philadelphia area (PECO). Even if I do have to make the first call to PECO's easily remembered 800 number when a tree falls and knocks down a line on our little street, after that, anticipatory behavior from the utility kicks in. The utility's automated messaging system lets me know if the problem has already been reported or if it needs me to provide more details, calls me back when the crew's on its way, and tells me the estimated time until power will be restored. This is exactly the information my family needs to know to plan our response to the situation.

In tornadoes and other severe circumstances, this becomes even more important. Government agencies have become accurate and proactive about issuing severe weather alerts, to the point that the risk from tornadoes within the United States has become, at least in theory, more a risk to property than to life. This is why the terrible loss of life in the May 2011 Joplin, Missouri, tornado is, at present, such a puzzle. While the physical damage to neighborhoods and commercial areas was unavoidable, what's disturbing here is that the emergency alert systems failed to get humans to shelter, in a way that wasn't supposed to happen. "'Something didn't work the way we'd like it to,' says Harold Brooks, a research meteorologist with the National Severe Storms Laboratory in Norman, Oklahoma."[5] One theory is that the reason for the failure, although heightened by the odd timing of the storm (occurring as several proms let out), was the spamlike effect of excessive alerts: Too many previous warnings to too many nonaffected people had created numbness.

If you're working with customers, this numbness hazard is something you need to actively avoid, whether you deal in life-and-death situations or not. In the case of the weather agencies, they're responding to the issue by incorporating better targeting and less-spamlike behavior into their next round of improvements. The National Weather Service in the U.S. is in the process, as I write this, of unveiling a new Personal Localized Alerting Network. Once it's rolled out, any county will be able to broadcast a warning *specifically and exclusively* to cell phones in the threatened area, transmitted to those phones from the nearest cell tower. "Anybody with a bar on their cell phone in that tower's range—usually about 10 miles—will get the messages," says John Ferree, Severe Storms Service leader for the National Weather Service in Norman.[6]

## permission to anticipate

To be so electronically attentive to and proactive with your customers requires *permission*. I know this doesn't seem fair, considering that your purpose is to *help* customers, but just like the old joke about the psychiatrist (he can only change a lightbulb that *wants* to change), the customer has to want your proactive assistance—and you have to *know* the customer wants it. Here's why you need permission:

▶ No matter how justified you feel you are in contacting a customer, legally speaking you may still need permission to make that contact, depending on your business relationship and the jurisdiction in which you do business.

▶    Assuming you have *legal* permission, you need to be sure that you're following the *emotional* definition of permission laid out by master marketer Seth Godin, who invented the concept of permission marketing:

> Permission marketing is the privilege (not the right) of delivering anticipated, personal and relevant messages to people who actually want to get them.
>
> It recognizes the new power of the best consumers to ignore marketing. It realizes that treating people with respect is the best way to earn their attention.
>
> "Pay attention" is a key phrase here, because permission marketers understand that when someone chooses to pay attention they are actually paying you with something precious. And there's no way they can get their attention back if they change their mind. Attention becomes an important asset, something to be valued, not wasted.
>
> Real permission is different from presumed or legalistic permission. Just because you somehow get my email address doesn't mean you have permission. Just because I don't complain doesn't mean you have permission. Just because it's in the fine print of your privacy policy doesn't mean it's permission either.
>
> Real permission works like this: If you stop showing up, people complain, they ask where you went.
>
> I got a note from a *Daily Candy* reader the other day. He was upset because for three days in a row, his *Daily Candy* newsletter hadn't come. That's permission.[7]

Note that this may put you at loggerheads with some in your marketing department concerning how, and with what frequency, you'll make contact with customers. Amazon.com sends me an email every time my orders are placed, when my orders ship, and in the event of a delay or other problem with my order. Super. But this means I hear from it a *lot*, because I order from Amazon.com a lot. So Amazon.com gives me an option to alert the company to all the other times I *don't* want to hear from it. It's quite a long list:

> Musical Instruments /Books /General Offers /Software /Shoes / Office Products & Supplies/ Automotive /Baby /Beauty / Grocery /Health & Personal Care /Home, Garden & Pets / Sports & Outdoors /Tools & Home Improvement/Industrial & Scientific /Jewelry /Magazine Subscriptions /Music/Toys & Games /Video Games /Computer & Accessories /MP3 Downloads/Kindle /Video on Demand /Movies & TV /Electronics/ Watches/Amazon Partners /Clothing & Accessories /Associates[8]

Amazon.com offers a single-checkbox escape hatch to protect me here, a simple unsubscribe that frees me from *non*-transactional emails but still keeps me in the loop when I need to be:

> **Do not send me email.** *Check this box to stop receiving all Amazon.com communications (except transactional emails).*
> **Note:** *Even if you choose not to receive some marketing emails from us, you will still receive our transactional email, such as messages related to your orders . . .*[9]

Your marketing department may not have the same confidence in your customers that Amazon.com has in its customers. They may use any email or phone number that a customer volunteers as a potential receptacle for undifferentiated marketing materials. In addition, your systems may not be set up like Amazon.com's, allowing your customers to opt out of one stream (marketing) and not the other (transactional). If so, you have a problem to fix— pronto—because nothing can be taken away faster than permission, the permission you need to maintain in order to be anticipatory.

▶     You need specific permission and knowledge of how your customer wants to be reached. Consider the telephone. With so many customers listing only a cell phone as their point of contact, be careful: You call that number at your peril if you don't have permission. As pioneering social media maven and writer Peter Shankman (check out his book *Customer Service: New Rules for a Social Media World*) says, "Just because you have all of [a customer's] contact info doesn't mean you have the right to use it. (Try to sell me something by calling my mobile, and I'll crush you.)"[10]

On the other hand, texting or calling a mobile phone to give a customer a needed *alert* may be very well received. As with most things, the difference is in whether you've met the definition of *permission*. In an example that Price and Jaffe cite, two private health insurers asked their customers for a phone number as part of their sign-up form. The first insurer (Fund A) just asked for a phone number and later called the customer when it had a need. The second insurer (Fund B) offered the customer a checkbox, requesting permission to call and a preferred time of day.

> When Fund A called its customers, they were greeted with hostility: "I emailed you; why are you calling?" The insurer quickly dropped the idea, as it didn't want to annoy customers. Fund B, in contrast, called only those customers who had given permission (and the vast majority did), and these customers welcomed this service and were expecting the call.[11]

# the specific medium is the message—and its only chance of getting through

To call or text or not to call or text a customer's mobile is a rather easy decision to work out for each customer. But there are more technologically complex ones as well. These come down to finding out specifically how your customer likes to receive alerts: HTML, standard mobile formatting (a stripped down version that works well on a smartphone such as an Android-compatible phone or iPhone), or text-formatted, which is handy for an old-school BlackBerry and important for the visually impaired.

Platinum Hotel Las Vegas handles this quite well (you can visit micahsolomon.com to view screenshots of how Platinum does it). The hotel sends out automated alerts prior to a guest's arrival, checking that all details on the reservation and in the guest's preference file are correct. Each alert features a simple view-*switching* selection at the top—"view: HTML–Mobile–Text"—allowing the guest to switch the way information is displayed, regardless of what the guest may have *initially* indicated as a preference.

I recommend you consider offering this format-switching functionality front and center like Platinum does, because customers are nothing if not fickle. Anticipate that, too.

## "and your point is?"

▶  The predominant way businesses add to customer burdens is by wasting their time.

▶  Touch points with customers shouldn't be occurring because of broken processes; being made to call too many times for "stupid stuff" will drive your customers away.

▶  Misguided metrics can be hazardous to the success of your customer interactions. Specifically, limiting call time for CSRs is one of the top causes of repeat calls.

▶  Even if customers haven't *asked* you to eliminate "stupid stuff" for them, they still probably want you to. Amazon.com, Schwab.com, and other savvy organizations have frequently invented ahead of their customers by tracking the stupid-stuff calls and then mostly eliminating them via automated confirmations and other creative solutions, leaving staff free to handle the more complex and unusual issues that crop up.

► Applied properly, the principle of "getting to them first" is a way to use technology to make customers feel remembered, cared for, and, ultimately and paradoxically, left alone, knowing the company is handling everything that may come up.

► Make sure the automated alerts you send are accompanied by an opportunity for the customer to reach a human being if desired.

► To be electronically attentive to and proactive with your customers requires their *permission*— for legal reasons and to be effective. So be sure you're following the definition of "permission" laid out by Seth Godin: "Permission marketing is the privilege (not the right) of delivering anticipated, personal and relevant messages to people who actually want to get them."

► Nothing can be taken away faster than permission, and you need to maintain permission to aid your efforts to be anticipatory.

► You need to know how your customer wants to be reached. Find out how your customer likes to receive alerts: HTML, standard mobile formatting, etc. And make it easy for customers to switch their option.

# chapter 11

# anti-social media

## fears and hazards of the new landscape

**the question is inevitable and invariable:** It comes without fail at the end of one of my speeches/when I meet a new consulting client/ when my seatmate on the plane finds out what I do for a living. The question? *"What should I do about social media?"*

Let me first dive into the *undercurrent* contained in this questioning. I believe what people are really asking is, "Micah, isn't it *dangerous* out there for my brand, my company, myself, in social media land? Can my brand really survive out there, with the floodgates of social media opened? How do I even have a prayer in this new landscape where any fourteen-year-old with a grudge can damage a brand's reputation, and even the most unjustified, poorly articulated customer gripe gets a huge megaphone via Yelp, TripAdvisor, and similar user-generated sites?"

## bicycle pumps and veterinarians

Yes, it *is* dangerous out there. Social media can affect your public persona and your profit picture. But don't put the cart before the e-horse. Being an ace at social media won't make you excellent, or even moderately good, at providing customer service any more than knowing how to work a bicycle pump will turn you into a veterinarian. The basis for establishing sound and responsive customer service starts with *customers*, not media.

Furthermore, it's important to remember that the communications and connectivity revolution of recent years includes a lot more than social media. It spans mobile technology, the rise of web commerce in general, improvements in manufacturing and process design, advances in self-service, and more. So while social media commands most of the headlines at present, it's not clear what we'll be saying about the phenomenon a few years or even months from now, once social media has found its place in the communications mix.

In the meantime, though, there *is* danger out there. But like most dangers, it gets more manageable when you look at it in a straightforward manner—and tackle it head on.

## regime change in 140 characters

When Terry Gross of *Fresh Air* asked Twitter cofounder Biz Stone if he had ever imagined that his invention was going to be used to bring down regimes in the Middle East, Biz shot back to Terry in a facetious "Dr. Evil" voice: "Of course, absolutely, that was the plan all along."[1]

The reality, joking aside, is that Twitter and other social media tools *do* have the power to bring about regime change in the business world. The names of well-known companies that have experienced this could nearly fill a chapter by themselves.

## ouch: the first time they talk about *you*

Our concern, though, really isn't these household brands. What about *your* company? The first time you discover that your company's being discussed negatively online, it's a tense, anxiety-ridden situation. What you see may look something like this, a moderately fictionalized version of a rant that was posted on the online review site Yelp:

*The hostess here can't pronounce "carpe diem." I wouldn't mention her ignorance on this point—even though the name of HER RESTAU-RANT is "Carpe Diem"—if she hadn't left me waiting, spilled the drink she pressured me into ordering, refused to make eye contact, said "uh huh" instead of "You're welcome," . . .*
*But she did all that to me.*
*So I \*\*am\*\* mentioning it.*

Ouch. Obviously this mixture of cattiness, generalized consumer upset, and actual, useful feedback represents something new. The world has changed. The balance of power between customer and business has changed. The timetable needed to respond has changed.

And the issue isn't always limited to *words*, like those in this Yelp posting. Sometimes there are *photos* involved. Let's say your above-Yelped restaurant, Carpe Diem, has a crack between two tables where your waitstaff forgot to clean. No business owner wants to see an oversight like that exposed online via TwitPic or yfrog, two services that allow you to send out photos via Twitter, but it can happen.

Just getting used to *that* concept? What about candid *video*? Yeah, it's out there. And it can bite you in the social.

## nobody uses twitter to tell a friend his fly's undone

The first secret of dealing with social media feedback, even the ostensibly negative, is to realize the "bad" stuff is rarely *all* bad news. That's because social media is such a remarkable source of feedback—round-the-clock, real-time hard data and nuanced subjective impressions that you can use to improve your service. Unfortunately, the entire world can be listening in real time along with you, which is, as my kids would say, kind of suckish. So you need to be listening . . . faster. Improving more quickly than the rest of the world is listening.

The second reality of social media feedback is that it would be more comfortable to not receive that feedback at all—the harsher stuff at least—in an open forum. It's undeniable that it would feel nicer to have your customers voice their complaints to you directly and discreetly rather than hit the "airwaves" with them. So, the second secret of dealing with social media feedback is to *reduce the need for it* by making sure your customers know, as directly as possible, how to reach you. Think about it this way: If your friend saw you had your fly undone, would he *tweet* about it? No, he'd quietly tell you.[2] Use the same principle to your advantage here. Why should customers address issues to you *indirectly* via Twitter or their blogs when they can use email, the phone, or a feedback form on your website and know that it will be answered—*immediately?* (Or maybe a customer does go ahead and uses Twitter, knowing that you're monitoring that particular handle, à la Delta or Southwest, so regularly that he will have every reason to repost in delight when you respond to him immediately.) What you don't want your customers to feel is festering anger, frustration, fear, tension, or the old Capitol Hill construct "they left me twisting slowly in the wind."

With their round-the-clock access to the "airwaves," make sure that the first impulse of customers is to reach *you*—day or night. Have "chime in" forms everywhere; it's like building escape valves for steam into your machinery. (If you're Amazon.com or another online aggregator, with a vast product line that's supplied in large part by outside vendors, your sensitivity to open conversations will be lowered; your customers can let off steam with zero downside for your overall brand. But most of us, obviously, aren't Amazon.com. More about this in Chapter 13.)

In Chapter 2 I laid out the formula for customer satisfaction, starting with a "perfect product" and "caring delivery." In consideration of that framework, the key way to avoid impact from negative public feedback is to make sure you're doing so many things right (that your product is so perfect and your service so caring) that the occasional wrongs seem like outlying events. Exceptions to the rule. Freakish occurrences, even.

But post some people will, which brings us to the third pillar of addressing the realities of social media: You need to develop strategies for rapidly responding in a concerned, empathetic, nonconfrontational manner. We will go through this subject in detail in the next chapter (Chapter 12).

## social media is not a disease

Social media isn't a newly emerged exotic disease with no effective cure. The reality of the situation is that social media is most dangerous to your company when your organizational structure and culture are set up in a way that keeps you from providing one-on-one service and responses to issues in real time with great flexibility. Top-down decision making with a helpless, slavishly script-driven front line will kill you in the social media world. You need to push individual employee ability to act down the line to the actual people who work with customers.

## a story that *almost* became a viral tweet

Here's a story that *almost* became a widespread tweet. I include it here because I want to impress on you why it's become more important than ever to give elective power to employees, to hire those employees appropriately, and to build a pro-customer culture in your organization now that companies face a rush-to-tweet-your-frustrations world. When a company fails to offer employees flexibility and discretionary power, and lacks a culture that encourages employees to take the customer's side quickly, it risks great danger in the world of social commerce.

I bought an e-reader some fourteen months ago, choosing from the various options available on the market. Now, two or so months out of warranty, without any abuse to the unit that I know of, one morning the screen suddenly looked like a broken Etch A Sketch®, or more accurately, like an Etch A Sketch that someone has painstakingly drawn lines on of varying thicknesses up and down its entire length, making any text I try to read on it utterly illegible. Immediately, I sent a note, explaining the situation to the manufacturer. I expected the situation would be resolved immediately. After all, what company wants to be represented in the world by something so visibly problematic?

*Shows what I know.*

In a return email, the customer rep asked me for the order number, date of purchase, and serial number of the e-reader.

Hmmm.

I obligingly went through my old paperwork to find the order number. I copied the eentsy serial number off the back of the e-reader. All the while, I was figuring these were just formalities—part of the representative's attempt to figure out which refurbished or new model to ship me.

Five days later came the terse response: I could return the Etch-A Sketchified reader if I wanted and the company would send a replacement for $189 plus shipping (gotta love that final knife twist: plus shipping).

And what about my value as a customer—most obviously my purchase of dozens of books for the e-reader, as well as the background information that should've been visible in my file showing I'd been a good customer for various other products of theirs as well? Nothing I wrote to the customer service rep got through, because it didn't jibe with her received policy guidelines. It was as effective an interaction as trying to coax a change in facial expression from one of the guys on Mount Rushmore, the lowest point probably coming when she wrote "I hope you understand: *If we helped you out with this we'd have to help everyone.*"

Well, I wasn't going to put another $189 (correction: $189 plus shipping) in that company's coffers. And by not doing the exchange but instead holding onto the Etch A Sketch e-reader, I get to use it in my customer service presentations as probably my favorite visual illustration of how far off the rails customer service can go.

It's not a problem for a customer to tell a story like this in 140 characters when it's accompanied by a gory image uploaded to Twitter via TwitPic or yfrog. A story like this—ripe with outrage, visuals, pathos, even a bit of humor—is always ready to go viral.

So learn the principles in this book and you'll have less to fear from the itchy "send" fingers of your socially aware customers. Fail to learn them, and you'll be at their mercy.

## "and your point is?"

- ► The balance of power between customer and business has changed, and the timetable needed to respond has changed.

- ► The first secret of dealing with social media feedback is to realize that even the bad stuff is rarely 100% bad news because social media is such a remarkable source of feedback you can use to improve your service.

- ► The second secret of dealing with social media feedback is to reduce the need for it by making sure your customers know, as directly as possible, how to reach you 24/7, whether that's via email, the phone, or a feedback form on your website.

- ► The third part of dealing with social media is that you need to know and develop strategies for rapidly responding in a concerned, empathetic, nonconfrontational manner. This will be addressed in the next chapter.

- ► Social media is most dangerous to your company when your organizational structure and culture are set up in a way that keeps you from providing one-on-one service and responses to issues—in real time, with great flexibility.

# chapter 12

# social service

## principles for social media customer service

i'm going to start this chapter with a vote of support for my geekier friends, a concession, really: It's crucial to have technologically savvy people *supporting* your social media customer service work. These are in many ways revolutionary times, and the value of technical knowledge and aptitude can't be discounted. But while your tech wizards should be interacting with and involved in the team that handles your social media support, the people actually helming the operation and responding to customers need to be the same people who are involved in your day-to-day customer service operations and who are responsible for interacting with your customers.

While it's categorically untrue that being great at one thing (for example, working with technology) necessarily makes you poor at something else (e.g., interpersonal communication), there is, conversely, no reason to expect that a digitally brilliant person will necessarily have an affinity for customer support. Yet company after company I work with has tended by default to put these people at the head of their social media teams.

Your customer service experts need to know the new principles of social media, however. So hand them this chapter and let them flesh out their years or decades of customer know-how with these simple principles. This will go a long way toward creating the perfect combination.

## principle #1: avoid the fiasco formula: a digital stitch in time saves nine (million)

Can you spell F-I-A-S-C-O? The formula is:

Small Error + Slow Response Time = Colossal PR Disaster

That is, the magnitude of a social media uproar increases disproportionately with the length of your response time. Be aware that a negative event in the online world can gather social steam with such speed that your delay itself can become more of a problem than the initial incident. A day's lag in responding can be too much.

## principle #2: lie back and think of england: digital arguments with customers are an *exponentially* losing proposition

It's an ancient and immutable law: You can't win an argument with a customer. If you lose, you lose directly; if you win, you still lose—by losing the customer. But *online*, the rule is multiplied manifold because of all the *additional* customers you'll lose if they catch sight of the argument. So, you need to learn to lie back and think of the future of your company, as Victorian women were told to "lie back and think of England" to help them endure their marital duties. (There is a *lot* of lying back and thinking of England involved in doing your social media duties.)

If it helps you psychologically to get through it, try to remember that the people slamming your face in the social medialand toilet—the folks I call "Click Puppies"—are doing it *off the cuff*. *On the fly*. Unlike your staff and yourself, they're simply not acting like professional people at that moment when they mouth off in outrage. In fact, in many cases, after they've trashed you publicly online, they're off to something else, to their next nasty little 140-character haiku, with no memory of what they've done and how it may have affected you. Keep this in mind and try to move on to the next thing yourself as best you can.

## principle #3: turn twankers into thankers: reach out directly to online complainers

Okay, now that you're lying back, thinking your selflessly patriotic thoughts, fully restrained from flying off the handle, you can respond in a considered, positive manner. Principle #3 is a finesse move, so let's go through it step by step. Say you've spotted an outrageous tweet about your firm:

*Company X double-bills all customers—Must Think We R Suckrs—#FAIL*

How should you respond? If this twanker follows you on Twitter, that enables you to send him a direct message—so do it. Include a direct email address and direct phone number. If, however, said twanker isn't one of your followers, you'll need to figure out another way to reach him. How about replying publicly, on Twitter, listing your email address and expressing your chagrin and concern. (In an online forum such as a blog, TripAdvisor, or Facebook, you can respond in a similar manner, but through the comment mechanisms available there.)

In a scenario involving an upset customer, your ideal outcome, as I mentioned in the previous chapter, is to move the discussion out of a public venue and into a one-on-one situation, where you can work directly with your antagonist without thousands of eyes dissecting every move or, worse, catching bits and pieces as things progress, without ever grasping the whole story. This dispute resolution approach is like an in-store situation where you take an irate customer aside, perhaps into your office, to privately discuss the matter, giving you both a chance to work together to arrive at a resolution.

You don't ever want to appear to be cyber-stalking your customer, though. After a reasonable attempt at contact, leave the ball in the court of the posting customer. If he does return contact, this is your chance to make it clear to the customer *right away* that you're on his side. What's sure to be a failure is a courtroom approach, showing how much proof you have that you're right and he's wrong. Apologize and accept fault—immediately and fully. Satisfy the customer *plus* do something extra. Only then ask the customer—*as a favor, not as a demand*—to amend or even withdraw those original ugly comments.

### SLAPP-Happy: How *Not* to Respond to a Social Media Twanker

When someone attacks your business online, you may be tempted to call your lawyer. My field is business, not law—I don't even play a lawyer on Hulu—so I'm not technically qualified to dissuade you. But from what I've seen, legally threatening the twanker who made you feel so bad is going to fail as a strategy for addressing customer complaints, for two reasons.

First, it may be illegal. A "SLAPP" lawsuit is a "strategic lawsuit against public participation." "Strategic" in that you don't expect to go to court; you intend to silence your critic and discourage other critics. But this strategy is illegal, as far as I can determine, in twenty-six U.S. states, and in several other countries. Now, I know this is frustrating when your business has been unfairly slammed, and I agree that it's an open question whether these laws are working as intended. Anti-SLAPP legislation is designed to protect the free speech of "little guys," but it does nothing to defend the actual little guys in business against what can be the devastating consequences of treatment in the hands of heavy hitters like Yelp and Google Places.

Still, I suggest you hold your fire. Even if threatening your customer *doesn't* land you in legal hot water or with daunting bills for court costs, the entire approach is likely to end up SLAPPing you in the face. The reason? Your reaction tends to bring excessive publicity to the issue. There's even a term for this: the Streisand Effect, named after Barbra Streisand, who sued a photographer in a failed attempt to remove a photo of the singer's mansion from the California Coastal Records Project,[1] a strategic misstep that resulted in the infuriated photographer going out of his way to give the photo wide distribution that it would never have received before.

At the very least, the threat of legal action does nothing to reduce the damage. You don't have to be Streisand and your SLAPP-ee doesn't have to be a tenacious photographer for such a lawsuit or threatened lawsuit to end up backfiring. Look at the following hilariously written backhanded "retraction" by a restaurant guest under legal threat, and think if coercing a customer into such a response really serves your business. (I've renamed the restaurant and changed some culinary details below. Yelp, however, has shown no such compassion.)

> On March 3, I posted a review on this website and seven days later I was threatened with a lawsuit by an attorney representing "Serenity Café" for two unverified statements that I made . . . In order to peacefully resolve this matter I am following the course of action the attorney has requested in the letter:
>
> 1. I will retract my posting—Below is my written retraction
>
> 2. I will remove the posting—the posting is hereby replaced by this retraction
>
> 3. I will not make libelous statements about "Serenity Café."
>
> Retraction of my July 6th posting pertaining to "Serenity Café":
>
> I had no malicious intentions when writing this review . . . Nonetheless, in retrospect I really should have said "*To me,* the line-caught rainbow trout tasted like farmed fish because it was almost flavorless and it looked like farmed fish because it was the wrong color and crumbly. Perhaps it was indeed wild trout that just spent too long in the freezer . . ." and I should also have said pertaining to the chicken that . . ."this chicken *seemed to me* like frozen tenders because it was the *size, shape and texture of large pieces of solid plastic.*"[2]

◆ ◆ ◆ ◆ ◆

It's hard for me to add much to that "retraction" in words of warning or counsel. The message is clear: SLAPP-er beware.

## principle #4: consider getting a complainer on the telephone (with permission)—even if the relationship *started* in social media land

First a caution: Mostly, people expect to be contacted only through the channel in which they first made themselves known—especially if their relationship to your brand is new or superficial. A small-time Amazon Marketplace merchant who somehow obtains a customer's phone number, for example, will mightily surprise that customer with even the friendliest of telephone follow-ups regarding the discount camera battery she bought.

However, if you're a company that has a multichannel (email, phone, in-person) relationship with a customer but the relationship has constricted over time to email or social only, or if you're able to ask your customer in an email or via a Twitter DM (direct message) for permission to call, it can work well to jump on the phone to defuse tensions that were first voiced in a social media posting. The telephone has emotionally instructive cues (timbre, tempo, inflection) that are missing from anything keyboarded. Plus, many times a customer will be as grateful as you are to have the cycle of postings ended by an old-fashioned two-voices-on-the-phone exchange. Never discount the power of the simple telephone: Perhaps no piece of technology works better for helping you make a direct person-to-person connection and privately resolving a dispute with a customer. Once you've resolved the issue to your customer's satisfaction, with any luck, you can return to the much broader forum of social media to broadcast the happy outcome.

# principle #5: get happy outcomes into the public eye

Once you've worked things out directly with your complainant (and I mean *really* worked them out), *then* ask in a nondemanding way if she would consider deleting the tweet. Or, in a forum where deletion is not an option, you might ask the person to post the satisfactory results of your intervention. Often, the complaining customer will be quite willing to do that, although this may require you to engage in some follow-up; after you've made a good attempt at reconciliation or problem resolution, she'll welcome the opportunity to bury the hatchet. But don't ask too soon, and don't be too demanding about it. Persistent, yes; demanding, no. Appeal to the higher nature of your now-pleased customer.

# principle #6: use social media and personal email to make your customers feel important

As with nearly all things in customer service, making a customer feel important is key in social media. Here are some tips:

▶ **If someone follows you on Twitter, "likes" your company on Facebook, adds you to a circle on Google +, or does the equivalent in another forum, thank her.** And, depending on your company policy, follow/like the person or entity back. So that this approach doesn't get too unwieldy, you can filter people you follow using your Twitter client (the most popular Twitter clients are TweetDeck, now owned by Twitter itself, and Hootsuite); some filtering functionality is built right into Google +'s "circles."

▶ **If someone says something nice about you online, thank her for that publicly *and* privately.** The public thank-you is partly for your benefit (it gets the positive comment out there again); the private thank-you is to show additional gratitude to the positive poster.

> **More generally, use Twitter, Facebook, Google +, and email to thank your customers for their business, with relative frequency.** This improves your customer service through the act of communicating your gratitude and also by offering you a chance to improve based on the feedback you may receive when you reach out one on one.

> **Don't demand that customers think about you all the time.** Customer attention wanders. While you wish you could always bring the focus back to you, it's not realistic to bombard a customer or prospect with your messages. Doing so is your most direct route to an "unfollow," "unlike," or "unsubscribe."

## principle #7: monitor

It's no use being poised to properly address customer service issues if you never hear about them in the first place. Here are some ways to ensure you hear everything that's being said about your company:

> **Set up a wide range of Google Alerts to get your attention when any discussion of your company happens (google.com/alerts).** Monitor not only your company name but also any conceivable misspellings, abbreviations, and slang versions of it, as well as the names and misspelled names of prominent people at your company. Set your Google Alerts to come at rapid intervals (termed "as it happens"), rather than once a day. While good work habits would suggest you set them for "once a day" to avoid interruptions, to avoid a fiasco (see Rule #1), you sometimes need to get on issues faster than after up to a full day's lapse.

► **Search Twitter. You can do this in real time through your Twitter client (TweetDeck or Hootsuite).** Set up columns for your @ handle, your company name, any prominent people at your company, typical misspellings, hashtags that interest you (#mycompanyfail, or #ourcoolconference2013, for example), and so on, and monitor them frequently. You should also do a retrospective search on a regular basis at whatever the best Twitter search engine happens to be when this book is published. (Currently, it's a Google beta engine with an endlessly long and involved URL; find it by searching in Google for "Twitter search." The official Twitter search engine is limited but has a clean interface and is available at search.twitter.com.)

# principle #8: if your social responses are inferior to—or not integrated with—your other channels, they're *hurting* your brand

If you set up an expectation that you will assist, interact with, and engage customers through social media, then you need to do that, and do it fabulously. If you're not up for it, then *don't*. I could blow your mind by recounting the legions of immensely famous companies that don't understand this, from high-end department stores to airlines to manufacturing and other B2B operations. Just as your brand is only as good as its weakest employee, customer service is only as good as your weakest channel of customer communication. This involves Rule #7: Monitor—and most of all, it involves committed follow-through and upholding of standards. For example, making sure all departments in your company know of your social media forays firsthand and in detail (rather than hearing about them first from a customer) and making sure that spelling and language use and other niceties are heeded online as well as off, to keep them consistent with your brand as it's laid out in other channels.

# "and your point is?"

- ► You need technologically savvy people supporting your social media customer service work, but the people actually helming the operation and responding to customers need to be the same ones who are expert at day-to-day customer service operations and are responsible for interacting with your customers.

- ► When a concern is voiced online, the magnitude of a social media uproar increases exponentially with the length of the company response time.

- ► Of course, it's always been true that you can't win an argument with a customer. But online, the rule is *multiplied* manifold because of all the additional customers you'll lose if they catch sight of the argument.

- ► If it helps you to get through it, try to remember that those slamming you in social media–land (whom I term "click puppies") are doing so off the cuff. In many cases, after they've trashed you publicly online, they're off to something else.

- ► In a scenario involving an upset customer, your goal is ideally to move the discussion out of a public venue and into a one-on-one situation, where you can work directly with your antagonist without thousands of eyes watching every move.

- ► You don't ever want to appear to be cyber-stalking your customer. After a reasonable attempt at contact, leave the ball in the customer's court.

- ► Mostly, people expect to be contacted only through the channel in which they first made themselves known— especially if their relationship to your brand is new or superficial. However, jumping on the phone to defuse tensions first voiced in a social media posting can work great *if* you have a relationship with a customer that is multichannel (email, phone, in-person) but has become constricted over time to email or social only, or if you're able to ask in an email for permission to call.

➤ Only once you've worked things out directly with your complainant should you ever ask the customer (in a non-demanding way) to consider deleting the offending posting. (Or in a public forum where deletion is not an option, you might at that point ask the person to post the satisfactory results of your intervention.)

➤ Don't demand that customers think about you all the time. It's not realistic to bombard customers or prospects frequently with your messages unless you want them to unsubscribe from your emails or "unlike" you.

➤ Set up a wide range of Google Alerts, set to be delivered in real time, to get your attention when any discussion about or relevant to your company or its brands is going on.

➤ If your social media responses are inferior to—or not integrated with—your other channels, you're hurting your brand.

# chapter 13

# listening

## your ears are your most important technology

**to circle back to the theme** I introduced a bit raunchily at the start of Chapter 1, customer service can benefit from a lifetime of refinement of your technique. To move the discussion above the belt, the portion of customer service that could be termed *listening*, broadly defined to include hearing, sensing, interpreting, reviewing, and comprehending, is one area that can especially benefit from this lifetime of refinement: tuning your organization's ears, in other words. By hiring properly, you'll have (mangling my anatomical metaphor) started your ears off on the right foot: You'll have selected employees specifically for their level of empathy (the "E" in "WETCO"). This really is the enchanted point of entry. The natural strengths of these employees can then be toned through guidance from supervisors and from peers already embedded in a culture that values listening.

## only one perspective that matters

Not long ago, I had the chance to watch a skillful manager field a complaint from a guest who was hesitantly bringing up her concerns. Here's the customer (after describing a troubling interaction): "Of course, your employee may have a different perspective from mine on how this went down."

The manager's immediate response: "Ma'am, as far as we're concerned, *there's only one perspective that matters.*"

Which is a good way of looking at it. As a business, the primary perspective that matters to you, if you want to *stay* in business, is the customer's. Even when it's arguably a *mis*perception on the part of the customer, you need to hear that misperception, feel that misperception, own that misperception. Figure out how it can be avoided in the future, for other customers as well as this one, by aligning the perspective of your insiders (employees) to that of the outsiders (customers) you want to welcome in.

I don't want you to misapprehend this sentiment and take it to mean that the feelings and humanity of your *employees* don't matter. They matter enormously. They matter because:

▶ They affect how your employees *treat* customers.

▶ They affect how customers *feel* about your company, when you're high-touch like Hyatt: Consider the uproar, including boycott calls[1] and the passing of new legislation,[2] that occurred after the three Hyatt hotels in Boston fired their entire housekeeping staffs without notice, replacing them with outsourced temps lacking benefits or direct accountability. And when you're high-tech like Amazon.com, a company praised often in these pages and previously viewed by many customers as wholly benign, that suffered a change in public perception after investigative reporting revealed that more than a dozen workers in Amazon's Allegheny County, PA, warehouse suffered hospitalization-inducing heat exposure from warehouse temperatures of up to 114 degrees in the summer of 2011.[3] (Amazon.com responded to the heat and suffering by offering the workers "popsicles," "5 minute additional breaks," and "heat hardening training.")[4]

Employees are customers too. They know customers, they blog to customers, they're married to customers. It's a highly transparent world. You need to work with your employees, and for your employees, because they're who will create the ultimate customer perspective, whether bad, indifferent, or transcendent.

## sanctuary much: the s.m.a.r.t. approach to the human force field

Culture, employee selection, positive peer pressure—these are keys to developing your company's listening skills—its ears. And until you build this philosophical and human backdrop, specific training is less than fully effective. You can't "concentrate on the nuts and bolts" when you lack a framework. But detailed training is indeed very valuable once you have this framework, and the type of training likely to have impact includes both classroom-style learning and the role-playing and scenario-driven activities that challenge your employees as realistically and as aggressively as possible. One of the reasons that pre-training with realistic scenarios is important is because of a particular self-inflicted challenge: You've hired friendly people, and they'll be used to working with other friendly people, whom you've also hired. But not all customers are friendly all of the time. This is akin to how crowd-control troops are repeatedly pre-tested with provocations *before* heading in to face a crowd that will try to make them lose their cool; thus your "troops" need to be trained in possible customer reactions they may encounter and in responding in the best possible way.

Ultimately, let's face it: The situation of serving others is different from being served. As someone calling himself Ishmael puts it when signing on as a sailor in *Moby Dick*, "There is all of the difference in the world between paying and being paid." That inherent positional difference, compounded by any difference between employee and customer in temperament, time sensitivity, socioeconomic status, and more can wreak havoc if your team hasn't been through it all before and learned to think on their feet (or, to make a stab at keeping my physique-speak consistent, on their ears).

One of the points your training should convey is that *individual* customers are the backbone of business growth. This makes it important for your team to get good at sensing the extent to which your customer's individual protective shell or force field is open or closed at any particular moment. A proper training curriculum in anticipatory service helps staff members learn to recognize—anticipate—when and when not to venture near and into the customer's protective bubble, the invisible sanctuary within which the customer has expectations of solitude. Here are the principles of this human force field, forming my acronym SMART:

*S*tart: **The customer expects service to begin the moment she comes into contact with the staff person.** In person, a warm greeting should include eye contact and a smile. (A note for busy offices: Sometimes this needs to be accomplished even if your employee's on the phone or speaking with another customer; for example, a busy checkout/reception desk attendant may need to learn how to work with one customer while visually acknowledging the presence of a new arrival.)

*M*essages: **If you can read the messages customers are giving off, you'll know the level of service they want at any given moment, including "no service now."** For example, if a guest catches a server's eye, it may be merely accidental, but if the guest *holds* the server's gaze, it usually means he's expecting to be offered assistance.

*A*djust: **Staff members need to adjust to the pace of each customer.** Some customers are highly time-aware; others are as laid back as the day is long. This isn't detectable only in person, by the way: Cues can be discerned on the phone, in live online chat, via videoconferencing, etc.

**Re-order: Even if it inconveniences you, re-order your work activities to suit the customer's needs.** True service can never be slave to checking things off in a predetermined order on an employee's to-do list. Attending properly to a customer means adhering to the *customer's* schedule, not the other way around. The key, again, is to *listen*: If a guest is in the middle of proposing to his sweetheart, don't choose that moment to ask if his steak was cooked to the proper temperature!

**Terminate: Reseal the force field by terminating the encounter . . . or not?** At the apparent end of service, it's the service professional's responsibility to ask if anything additional is needed, and, if it isn't, to graciously thank the customer before leaving her in the sanctuary of her invisible force field. Again, this can apply in a chat sequence, a series of emails, or on the phone, as well as, of course, in person.

### Sticking Your Gooseneck Out

Patrick O'Connell's Inn at Little Washington is one of the few double Five Diamond Award–winning institutions (five diamonds for food, five diamonds for lodging—the top designation in both categories from AAA) in the country, and yet, rather than being the stuffy enclave you would expect from that designation, it's exactly as stuffy as a specific guest wants it to be. In the case of a guest like me, that means not very stuffy at all.

My manufacturing operation was for years one of the few businesses other than The Inn that was located in the tiny, isolated town of "Little" Washington, Virginia. And because there's no fast food for twenty miles in any direction, my wife and I felt we could save up what would've been our McDonald's money and every so often dine at The Inn as a splurge. (That's the story we told ourselves, anyway.) So the two of us arrived there one evening and decided on the tasting menu option, where The Inn suggests a specific "program" of food and wine for the evening. My wife was happy to order everything exactly as suggested, but I asked to substitute one course: I wanted an alternative to the *foie gras*. The waiter chatted with me for a moment and figured out I was declining the *foie gras* because of ethical concerns, but he also quickly got the sense that I was a guest who could take a joke at my own expense.

"Mr. Solomon, I can assure you: After one bite you'll agree this goose's liver was abused for a very good cause, as, in fact, we will be abusing *your* liver as the evening progresses. No chance I can change your mind?"

It was a perfect comeback. A moment like that can become fraught for a diner: all those articles in the *Times* food section warning you not to second-guess the chef by making substitutions, concerns of looking self-righteous or of embarrassing your date . . . but through his comment, the waiter was signaling "We are going to be here a *long* time together, my friend; let's get comfortable." Any potential awkwardness dissolved, and although I assuredly didn't give in and order the *foie gras* (I'm pretty sure the waiter knew I wouldn't), the evening was off to a great start.

# using electronic systems to enhance your listening

In commerce that incorporates self-service, a customer can set things up for himself by entering helpful personal details, a theme I've touched on earlier. This is a valuable type of electronic "listening"—or maybe it should be termed "recording"—and is an option expected by many of today's customers. It's a good way to avoid typos and to allow the entry of information that can be hard for a service provider to get right in all its nuances, such as instructions to leave packages under the left-hand side of the back porch if nobody is home. At my company, Oasis, the "my account" system we've built allows customers, if they like, to enter this kind of information and to update it 24/7 from whatever time zone they reside in.

Another element of electronic listening is to build "listening devices" into your communications with customers. Here are some examples:

- Surveys aren't only a chance to gather statistical data but also an opportunity to hear from individual customers and to respond quickly, and when the survey format is electronic it makes it possible for this interaction to happen nearly in real time. Make this your operating philosophy and make your philosophy clear in the survey's language. In other words, inform the person filling out the survey that individual input is both invited and will be responded to promptly. (More on this below, under "Surveying the Landscape.")

- FAQ-style self-service and automated messaging are, again, improved when you add an option to them that allows the customer to reach a human being when desired.

- Sometimes you may want to send out, with no further marketing bent or statistical goal in mind, an unadorned invitation to customers to speak their minds. At my company, for years I've sent out an invitation like this by email, from my "President and Founder's Desk," to each prospective customer, as a follow-up to the more marketing-directed emails our customers receive. Without any other agenda, this letter invites the recipient to sound off to me with anything on her mind.

  This kind of correspondence, of course, has to be handled carefully: It should include chances to opt out, and most important, when customers *respond* to the email, those responses should come directly to you (as they do to me), and you should be ready to review and reply. With many companies, by contrast, when a customer responds to one of the company's directly worded auto-emails, what happens? *Nothing.* This is one of the fastest credibility killers there is. For example, as a prospective customer, I recently tried an online backup service for my computer. When the thirty-day trial was up, I received a note, signed by the data storage company's CEO, sporting the bail bondsmanesque headline "Your Trial Is Up—What Happened?" and continuing on in this vein and tone. I replied to the email, explaining the specific reasons I hadn't signed on after the free trial and how the company could turn the situation around and win my business. What response did my note receive? *Nothing.* Apparently the email had been sent out under the assumption that I would go back to the site and re-up through the normal channels. But an email like this should be sent out as a *listening device*, with the sender waiting to listen with open ears to any customer or prospect who's interested enough to respond.

One of the best areas for enhanced listening and for creating anticipatory magic is where the lines intersect between electronic systems and human service. This requires you to have your humans and your systems working together in harmony. When this junction is well thought out, and handled with a nimble touch, you have an especially good chance to make your customer feel that everything's taken care of, that there's no need to explain oneself, that everything's *anticipated*. For example, if the technological systems of a great hotel are working in alignment with an empathetic and properly trained staff, magic can happen. A friend —the well-travelled CEO of an engineering firm, not someone easily impressed—experienced this not long ago:

> We arrived at a hotel in a rural Swiss town one afternoon—a hotel of significant size—and that evening had dinner in its restaurant, a very elegant place with a fine wine list and great service. The next evening we wanted to have a glass of wine in our room before going out to a different restaurant. I dialed room service and told the gentleman who answered that I would like to order a bottle of wine to be brought to our room. The gentleman said immediately, after using my name to address me, "Would you like the same wine you had

last night?" While he of course had accessed my name based on the room number I'd called from, to know that we had been in the restaurant, had ordered wine, and which particular wine, was quite a remarkable feat—especially in a hotel of at least 150 rooms operating close to capacity.[5]

Close communication and note-taking by the staff in different areas of the facility made this experience possible, and the contrast here to typical organizational siloing resulted in a transcendent service moment. I doubt my friend would have been as enchanted by the experience if he himself had been required to scour a wine list for last night's wine selection, then request the wine by name. There's something captivating about the human service experience, as long as humanity isn't used as an excuse to resist employing the best of processes and technology.

## Mispersonalized Customer Service

An awkward little meme is sweeping through hotel guest service operations at this very moment—and I mean *really nice* hotels that are eager to do well by their guests. It's unfortunate, because it makes customer service *less* personal in the course of a clunky attempt to personalize it.

I call the front desk from my room phone (I'm traveling alone). Before I say a word into the mouthpiece, here comes the response: "How may I assist the Solomon *party*?" But the Solomon *party* doesn't need any help; there's no party going on in here. On the other hand, *I* traveled a fair distance to stay here and am eager for some assistance.

Here's why this difference matters: As we've been discussing, personal service depends on *listening*—on setting up more, and more effective, ways to *hear* the customer. But doing that takes forethought. And sometimes it takes time. In this particular instance, it requires only a *moment* of extra listening time. By waiting until I say a single phrase in my (arguably) masculine voice, the hotel operator would be equipped to then reply, "Mr. Solomon, good evening," or "Mr. Solomon, I would be delighted to help you with that."

That allows you to provide service that is *personal*, not faux-personalized. And it's simple to pull off. You just have to be listening.

## it's all about listening—and it starts by opening yourself to hearing

Who in your company should do customer service? "Everyone" has always been my intentionally provocative answer. Now, I want to ask a similar question: Who should help you *improve* your customer service? Again, I'd suggest the answer is "everyone." This includes those inside *and* outside your company. We all live in what could be termed a Wiki-World, where the best answers often come from crowdsourcing (i.e., involving as many interested people as possible, rather than only a handful of experts).

Involve your employees and involve your vendors, as Zappos has with its extranet (Chapter 5), and you'll have a great start. If you can also involve your customers, that's even better, with potentially hundreds or thousands of eyes out there helping you find the right direction. While you have your feet up on your desk, or toes in the sand, if you prefer, these stakeholders can be populating your wiki and improving your knowledge base with a remarkable degree of sophistication. Subject, of course, to security and privacy protocols.

## the maytag repairman lets you slap him in the facebook

Let's look at how electronic listening techniques can help to rehabilitate a damaged brand, in this case Maytag. The lamentable backstory: Maytag, that formerly pristine American brand with an iconic lonely repairman, tarnished its nameplate when Whirlpool purchased the brand, moved its manufacturing overseas, and overlaid a service culture that was, shall we say, less than responsive. If that Maytag repairman felt any of his trademark pangs of loneliness in recent years, maybe they resulted from hiding in his office from the mounting complaints and online rants.

Including those of Heather P. Armstrong of Dooce, a much-read blog that's funny and insightful on a variety of subjects and has a fiercely loyal following. Despite many calls from Armstrong, and many ineffective repair attempts, Maytag continued to prove unable to provide her with a workable clothes washer. She finally called Maytag and warned that she was going to recount the entire experience on her blog and on Twitter. The now-legendary response from the Maytag representative: "Yes, I know what Twitter is, and no, that will not matter." Armstrong's exasperated response, on Twitter, to her thousands of followers: "So that you may not have to suffer like we have: DO NOT EVER BUY A MAYTAG. I repeat: OUR MAYTAG EXPERIENCE HAS BEEN A NIGHTMARE."[6]

To the company's credit, though, this isn't where the story ends. Whirlpool/Maytag realized that Twitter *did* matter, and it responded to Armstrong's post the way a savvy company would do when confronted with a high-powered critic, sending Jeff Piraino, manager of the executive offices of Whirlpool Corporation in Michigan, to work everything out. (From Ms. Armstrong's account, he did a splendid job.)[7]

And in a more interesting development, the company instituted a powerful long-term solution: *an online listening device.* Whirlpool, now the parent company of the Maytag, KitchenAid, and of course Whirlpool appliance brands, realized that the *next* situation like this should never reach a similar phase of escalation. And that the Heather Armstrongs of the world were potentially the brand's best friends, most cost-effective focus groups, best crowdsourced product designers, and biggest source of word-of-mouth marketing. So they stopped circling the wagons and shooting back at—or at best ignoring—those outside the wagon train

Whirlpool set up, monitors, and responds to Facebook pages for its three brands, pages where customers can really let the company have it. Check out, for example, the Facebook page for Whirlpool's "Discussions" forum (currently the URL is http://www.facebook.com/ Whirlpool?sk = app_2373072738; if that's changed by the time you receive this book, just go to http://www.facebook.com/Whirlpool and click on the "Discussions" link). Discussion topics (actual threads that various customers chime in on) run the gamut:

- ► Big thank you for wonderful, quick customer service

- ► Terrible products

- ► We like our appliances

- ► Disgusted with my Cabrio Washer

- ► Side-by-side fridge dead after six months

- ► Bad experience

These threads help the company address specific complaints and suggestions; as a fringe benefit, concentrating so much Whirlpool brands–related activity in one place improves the company's SEO (search engine optimization), ensuring that the Whirpool site, rather than Yelp, Complaints Board, or the like, will be what comes up first for its brand names on Google, allowing the company to respond on its own terms. Example: Here's a typical company response from the "Terrible Products" discussion thread. (Note that Jennifer from Whirlpool is restrained due to the customer's privacy settings from directly contacting the customer, which is why her response is phrased in the following manner.)

```
Dear [user name],
     I'm very sorry to learn your hot water heater quit
working, and I regret to learn of your experience with
customer service. I would like to contact you for more
```

```
information . . . Please send a message to my personal
account with your contact and appliance information.
```
```
Thank you,
Jennifer
```

# break it to ourselves more gently

One advantage to encouraging public outpourings, à la Whirlpool or Amazon.com, is that customers stop stewing like they're sealed inside a pressure cooker. The lid, in effect, has been taken off. Hate something about a product Amazon.com sells?—*say* something about that product, right there on the Amazon.com site. Amazon.com doesn't mind; it wants to retain you as a customer, unencumbered by those bad feelings you just let go of.

Of course, most of us aren't Amazon.com. We have smaller product lines, very dear to our hearts. Most of us aren't as bold as the Whirlpool brands, either: We would rather handle customer service more discreetly than is allowed by an open and messy airing on Facebook; we would prefer to hear *in private* about our failings, as I discussed in Chapter 11. Still, we need to listen, because *if we don't hear about issues now, we are going to hear about them later*—all over the internet. So if you're not encouraging public disclosure à la Whirlpool, or à la Amazon.com and its multiple imitators, you still need to publicize methods that customers can use to contact you. Every time a button on your site fails to work, you want your customers to know you're eager to hear about it via web form or email. When an instruction in your PDF-formatted user's manual proves too confusing, you want your customer to tell you about it via a live link to your chat operators, embedded in that PDF. Each time a customer in a different time zone receives a shipment from you and has trouble with your product, you sure as heck need to have communication channels open to receive those concerns—or you need to stop shipping to different time zones.

# surveying the landscape

Look to get the most out of every communication you send. Many can do double duty by also serving as a listening device. For example: surveys. I touched on surveys briefly above; let's go deeper. First off, how do you get people to even *fill out* surveys? At my company, we offer a donation to a relevant charity in honor of every customer who fills out a survey, and at the end of each year we publicize how much has been donated and by how many customers. This approach cuts very well through the marketing clutter. What do you ask on a survey? Of course, *you ask what matters to you:*

▶ **First, the overall impression: Whether customers love doing business with your company.** Use whatever words you wish to express this sentiment, but that's the essence of what you want to find out first. Why ask a question in this vein first? Because if you save it 'til the end of the survey, the picky little questions customers have answered already on the survey will color how they respond to this all-critical summary question. Note that sometimes this "do you love us" query is best phrased as a cluster of questions, for example:

1. How delighted were you?

2. How likely are you to return?

3. How likely are you to recommend us to your friends and colleagues?

▶ **Questions that have operational significance**, being sure not to ask them in your own operational jargon; always phrase them the way your customer will have experienced your service. Remember, your customer doesn't care about—and likely doesn't understand—your organizational chart and internal terminology, so "How did you feel about our IT department?" or "How do you feel about our catering staff?" are close to meaningless questions. By contrast, "Were the technical issues you encountered corrected to your satisfaction?" or "Was your tray picked up within thirty minutes of you leaving it outside your door?" are meaningful questions.

In addition (and this is the central reason for discussing this here), your survey needs to include multiple opportunities for your customers to let loose, knowing that you're listening. In addition to answering what *you're* curious to know, let your survey subjects tell you what's on *their* minds, *then get back to each of them personally.* This is one of the most effective ways to grow your business, customer by customer, as well as heading off any potential negative escalation.

Okay, I've got you listening—on the phone, in surveys, in person. But are you *capturing* the meat in the responses you receive? If you're not doing anything long-term and strategic with this data, at the very least *do something with it during the course of the customer's interaction with you.* In other words, when a CSR receives a call from a frustrated customer, flags need to go up so that if it's beyond that CSR's ability to handle, someone else can step in immediately, *and* so the situation is followed up on shortly to ensure it was resolved in a way that pleased the customer. If your product or service has a significant time-based element (a contract executed in phases, a product that takes time to ship, a hotel stay), a frustration early in the process needs to be noted and then acted upon later in the stay, with additional kindness and acknowledgment of what was suffered. This real-time element is a significant part of the value that high-quality listening, combined with high-quality systems, can bring to an organization.

But what I also encourage is for you to make use of this information to enhance *future* visits, calls, and purchases: to ensure continuity and a sense of being remembered for each returning customer. *There should be no sense of having to start over* for a customer returning to your company.

If a customer has to start over each time she works with your company, she may as well start over somewhere else.

Noting information, keeping it at the fingertips of employees involved in a customer interaction, and collating it properly for quick access in future visits are key parts of providing anticipatory service. They're at the heart of great brands, online or offline, high-tech or otherwise. So what is the information you want to include in a client file? *Whatever is important to that client.* If a customer shares information with you online (e.g., in the guest's two hundred character comment made in the course of reserving a hotel room online), have that customer input at the fingertips of your staff. The guest keyed it in, so he expects you to see it. In my business, if a client has won a particular film award at an independent film festival, I know that information matters to him; therefore, it matters to me. It's noted in his file, and the various staff members who work with him can see that notation, regardless of their position in my company.

It all comes down to not having to reinvent the ear each time a customer interacts with you. Cultivate great people, great online systems, and great self-service, and then collate the data properly. E-listening and plain old classic listening: These are your keys to anticipation.

♦ ♦ ♦ ♦ ♦

Now, I offer you *my* ears. Let me hear from you what you're missing in your business. What I've written here that you need clarified. What you're seeing out there that's frustrating or perplexing you. Write to me at micah@micahsolomon.com and visit me at www.customerserviceguru.com for more tips and resources, as well as photographs that illuminate points in this book. Or call me directly on my mobile phone: (484)343-5881. I'm all ears.

## "and your point is?"

> ▶ You've hired friendly people, and they'll be used to working with other friendly people. But not all customers are friendly,

all of the time, so provide training that includes classroom-style learning *and* role-playing and other realistic scenario-driven activities that challenge your employees in the same ways that customers may challenge them on the job.

▶ Your training needs to get across that *individual* customers are the backbone of business growth. A big part of this is training your team to sense when your customer's individual shell or force field opens and closes around her: when and when not to venture into the invisible sanctuary within which the customer has expectations of solitude.

Follow the principles of the human force field, using my acronym SMART:

**S**tart

**M**essages

**A**djust

**R**e-order

**T**erminate encounter . . . or not?

**S***tart:* The customer expects service to begin the moment she comes into contact with the staff person. In person, a warm greeting should include eye contact and a smile.

**M***essages:* If you can read the messages customers are giving off, you'll know the level of service they want at any given moment, including "no service needed right now."

**A***djust:* Staff members should adjust to the pace of each customer.

**R***e-order:* Even if it inconveniences you, re-order your work activities to suit the customer's needs. True service should never be slave to checking things off in order on a server's to-do list.

**T***erminate:* Reseal the protective shell by terminating the encounter . . . or not? At the apparent end of service, it's the service professional's responsibility to ask if anything additional is needed, and, if not, to graciously thank the customer before leaving him in his invisible sanctuary.

► An important element of electronic listening is to build "listening devices" into your electronic communications with customers:

- The best automated messaging and FAQ-style self-service include options that allow you to directly reach a human being.

- Online surveys are not only a chance to gather statistical data but also an opportunity to hear from individual customers and to respond quickly.

► One of the best areas for enhanced e-listening and for creating anticipatory magic is where the lines intersect between electronic systems and human service, provided you have the two of these working in harmony.

► Consider becoming a wiki-friendly company, allowing input from employees, customers, and vendors to bolster your knowledge base.

► One advantage to encouraging public outpourings is that customers with negative opinions can stop feeling the frustration of stewing without an outlet.

► If you're not going to encourage public, sometimes negative, disclosure on your sites in the manner of Whirlpool and of Amazon.com and its multiple imitators, you need to publicize methods for customers to contact you directly.

► What do you ask on a survey? First (using whatever words you wish to express this sentiment), ask whether your customer loves doing business with your company, and then ask questions that have operational significance. Your survey also needs to include opportunities for your customer to let loose—knowing you'll respond.

➤ Whether or not in the long run you're doing anything with the data collected from your listening efforts, *at the very least* do something with it during the course of the customer's interaction with you.

➤ If your product or service has a significant time-based element (a contract executed in phases, a product that takes time to ship, a hotel stay), a customer frustration early in the process needs to be noted so you can act appropriately later in the interaction based on this information.

➤ Transcribing information, keeping it at the fingertips of employees involved in a customer interaction, and collating it properly for quick access in future visits are key parts of providing anticipatory service.

➤ Now, I offer you *my* ears. Write me at micah@micahsolo mon.com for a direct response. Visit me at www.customer serviceguru.com. Call me directly on my mobile phone: (484)343-5881. And thank you.

# Notes

## introduction

1. Textual and geographic characteristics have been altered to avoid identification. The original was *at least* this extreme.

2. Richard Wiseman, *59 Seconds: Think a Little, Change a Lot* (Borzoi Books, New York, 2009), p. 140.

3. If you're reading the footnotes, you must be the thorough type. So, if you must know: Yes, there was exactly the correlation you might expect.

4. If wandering forests for old fencing and foundations isn't your thing, you can do it in your armchair in the excellent discussion of these mid-nineteenth-century changes in Bill Bryson's *At Home: A Short History of Private Life* (Doubleday, New York, 2010).

## chapter 1

1. Accenture Newsroom, "Use of Smartphones by Bargain-Hunting Consumers Is Changing the Customer-Retailer Relationship, Accenture Survey Finds," http://newsroom.accenture.com/article_print.cfm?article_id=5109.

2. Unfortunately, Amazon.com may be pursuing this need for speed at the expense of the workers who fulfill these orders, an

approach that's problematic if a company's striving to build a great company culture. Read the Sidney Award–winning exposé here: http://www.mcall.com/news/local/amazon/.

3. "The New Consumer Behavior Paradigm: Permanent or Fleeting?" 2010 PricewaterhouseCoopers LLP/ Kantar Retail.

4. Andrew Adam Newman, "A Direct Approach to Disaster Relief From Procter & Gamble," *New York Times,* quoting study by PR firm Edelman, June 3, 2011, p. B3.

5. Leigh Buchanan, "Decoding the New Consumer," *Inc.,* September 2010, p. 159.

6. Ibid.

7. Emily Weinstein, "All That Authenticity May Be Getting Old," *New York Times*, October 27, 2011, Home & Garden section.

# chapter 2

1. Alan Levin, "No U.S. Airline Fatalities in 2010," *USA Today,* January 21, 2011, http://travel.usatoday.com/flights/2011-01-21-RWaircrashes20_ST_N.htm.

2. AirSafe.com, "Recent Fatal Plane Crashes and Other Significant Airline Safety Events," http://www.airsafe.com/events/last_15.htm (last reviewed 10/30/11).

3. Alain de Botton, *A Week at the Airport: A Heathrow Diary* (Vintage Books, New York, 2009).

4. Tom Peters, *Liberation Management: Necessary Disorganization for the Nanosecond Nineties* (Ballantine Books, New York, 1994), pp. 682–683.

5. Jimmy Kimmel, "A Dramatic Story, at the End of Which Nothing Happens,"*Huffington Post,* March 14, 2011, http://

www.huffingtonpost.com/jimmy-kimmel/jimmy-kimmel-tsunami__835389.html.

# chapter 3

1. Which, with nifty circularity, was inspired by the early practices and writings of Henry Ford.

2. Another benefit to the company, of course, is the value these perks add in employee hiring and retention.

3. Proust's letter is cited in Alain de Botton, *How Proust Can Change Your Life* (Knopf Doubleday Publishing Group, New York, 1998).

4. I'm not in any way suggesting you skirt overtime rules, incidentally. My point is rather the opposite.

# chapter 4

1. Thanks to John Jantsch of Duct Tape Marketing for sharing this phrasing with me.

2. Apple is number three as of this writing for customer service of any company in *any* industry, according to the annual J.D. Power Bloomberg survey: http://www.businessweek.com/interactive_reports/customer_service_2010.html.

3. As Mike Wittenstein points out in his excellent white paper on the Apple retail experience "You Had Me at Hello," http://www.mikewittenstein.com/download/general-files/Apples_Customer_Experience_Secrets_2011.pdf.

4. Ibid.

5. See p. 52, Leonardo Inghilleri and Micah Solomon, *Exceptional Service, Exceptional Profit: The Secrets of Building a Five-Star Customer Service Organization* (AMACOM Books, New York, 2010).

6. As this book is going to press, Google just announced that the fate of some of these innovations is up in the air, due to Google's winding down of its innovative Google Labs.

# chapter 5

1. Scott Martin, "How Apple Stores Rewrote the Rules of Retailing," *USA Today,* May 18, 2011. http://www.usatoday .com/tech/news/2011-05-18-apple-retail-stores_n.htm.

2. Barbara Talbott, "The Power of Personal Service," Cornell University School of Hotel Administration/The Center for Hospitality Research, September 2006, http://www.hotel school.cornell.edu/research/chr/pubs/perspective/perspec tive-14183.html.

3. Isadore Sharp, *Four Seasons: The Story of a Business Philosophy* (Portfolio, New York, 2009).

4. Gretchen Morgenson, "Some Bankers Never Learn," *New York Times,* Business section, July 31, 2011.

5. You can get a vivid glimpse of the fiasco's origins via Chicago Public Radio's "This American Life," available as a podcast for free (but do contribute at pledge time). Start with the episode "The Giant Pool of Money," done in collaboration with Planet Money and the winner of a Peabody, http://www.thisameri canlife.org/radio-archives/episode/355/the-giant-pool-of-money.

6. Talbott, op. cit.

7. Anthony Lane, "The Fun Factory: Life at Pixar," *The New Yorker,* May 16, 2011, A Critic at Large.

8. There's an excellent discussion of this in Daniel H. Pink's *Drive: The Surprising Truth About What Motivates Us* (Riverhead, New York, 2009).

9. Leigh Buchanan, "A Customer Service Makeover," *Inc.*, March 2011, http://www.inc.com/magazine/20110301/a-customer-service-makeover.html.

10. Tina Rosenberg, *Join The Club: How Peer Pressure Can Transform the World* (W. W. Norton & Co., New York, 2011).

11. Tony Hsieh, *Delivering Happiness: A Path to Profits, Passion, and Purpose* (Business Plus, New York, 2010).

12. Not that I'm saying all is always rosy with *Keiretsu*, where suppliers' allegiances become entwined in a web that is hard to unwind. For more on the pros and cons of *Keiretsu*, it's worth looking at the rise of Carlos Ghosn and his rehabilitation of Nissan, a subject I wish I had room for here.

13. Wording is fictionalized slightly to avoid specific identification, on the off chance anyone still cares.

14. Raini Hamdi, "Horst Schulze: Defining the New Luxury," ehotelier.com, October 20, 2006, http://ehotelier.com/hospitality-news/item.php?id=A9500_0_11_0_M.

15. Isadore Sharp, *Four Seasons: The Story of a Business Philosophy* (Portfolio, New York, 2009).

16. Kelly Hodgkins, "The Secrets of Apple's Retail Success," *TUAW* (blog), June 15, 2011, http://www.tuaw.com/2011/06/15/the-secrets-of-apples-retail-success.

17. Tom Peters, "Excellence Always," August 21, 2008, www.tompeters.com/slides/uploaded/NewMaster090508_Part_1-3.ppt.

18. Lucas Conley, "Cultural Phenomenon," *FastCompany*, April 1, 2005, http://www.fastcompany.com/magazine/93/cultural-phenom.html.

19. Joe Nocera, "The Sinatra of Southwest Feels the Love," *New York Times*, May 24, 2008, Talking Business column.

20. "2010 Southwest Airlines One Report," http://www.south
    west.com/html/southwest-difference/southwest-citizenship/
    one-report.html.

21. Larry passed away before press time. Here is a memorial site,
    with clips of him speaking as well: http://drivingvision.com/
    wordpress/.

22. AZCentral.com, "Airline Workers Helped Save Guide Dog,"
    July 20, 2007, http://www.azcentral.com/arizonarepublic/
    business/articles/0720biz-buzz0720.html#.

23. The Colbert-Banner-Southwest story is featured on Beth
    Terry's blog *The Cactus Wrangler*, http://cactuswrangler.com/
    2007/07/16/southwest-airlines-employees-save-seeing-eye-
    dogs-life/.

24. Raymond Davis and Alan Shrader, *Leading for Growth: How
    Umpqua Bank Got Cool and Created a Culture of Greatness*
    (Jossey-Bass, New York, 2007), p. 116.

# chapter 6

1. Personal conversation with Michele Livingston, July 26, 2011,
   Seattle, Washington.

2. Raymond Davis and Alan Shrader, op. cit.

3. Alain de Botton, *A Week at the Airport*.

4. Marilyn Suttle and Lori Jo Vest, *Who's Your Gladys: How to
   Turn Even the Most Difficult Customer into Your Biggest Fan*
   (AMACOM Books, New York, 2009), p. 20. Questioner
   referred to is Robert Spector.

5. Talbott, op. cit., quoting Isadore Sharp's Singapore Workforce
   Development Agency *Leadership Forum Address*, October 27,
   2005.

6. Read more at wholefoodsmarket.com/careers/hiringprocess
.php.

7. Max Chafkin, "The Zappos Way of Managing," *Inc.*, May 1,
2009, http://www.inc.com/magazine/20090501/the-zappos-
way-of-managing_pagen_5.html.

8. Ibid. You may also enjoy the following colorful, if fermented,
references:
> http://www.ideaowl.com/blog/2011/06/5-things-i-
> learned-at-zappos-awesome-las-vegas-hq-tour/; http://
> www.geekatsea.com/inside-zappos-headquarters;, http://
> blogs.zappos.com/taxonomy/term/8458; http://
> www.deliveringhappiness.com/through-the-
> eyes-of-our-editor/.

9. *Harvard Business Review,* Blog Network, Bill Taylor July 12,
2011, http://blogs.hbr.org/taylor/2011/07/how_do_you_
know_a_great_person.html.

10. Peter Carbonara, "Hire for Attitude, Train for Skill," *Fast
Company,* August 31, 1996, http://www.fastcompany.com/
magazine/04/hiring.html.

11. Personal correspondence with Michael Hyter, July 20, 2011.
More on Hyter's work at www.globalnovations.com.

## chapter 7

1. Bruce Horovitz, "Applebee's, Olive Garden Face PR Problem
After Serving Alcohol to Kids," *USA Today,* p. B1, April 15,
2011.

2. Sontaya Rose, "Fresno Mom's Death: Dangerous Dosing
Levels Revealed," ABC News Fresno, April 11, 2011, http://
abclocal.go.com/kfsn/story?section = news/local&
id = 8065801_.

3. There's a great discussion of this in Daniel H. Pink's *Drive: The Surprising Truth About What Motivates Us* (Riverhead, New York, 2011).

4. The most famous of these studies was conducted in a nursing home and demonstrated that providing autonomy can be a question of life or death: "The debilitated condition of many of the aged residing in institutional settings is, at least in part, a result of living in a *virtually decision-free environment*" [emphasis mine]. By giving those residents responsibility—decision-making power and something to be in charge of—their health was actually improved, while the decision-free group's health continued to falter, to a very dangerous degree. (Ellen J. Langer and Judith Rodin, "The Effects of Choice and Enhanced Personal Responsibility for the Aged: A Field Experiment in an Institutional Setting." *Journal of Personality and Social Psychology*, 34(2) (1976): pp. 191–198.)

5. Hsieh, op. cit.

6. Hsieh, op. cit. on social media restrictions during Amazon acquisition; informal discussion with Zappos employees on restriction of photography due to potential tweeting and on related employee restrictions.

7. She's Joanne Hassis, Nordstrom, King of Prussia, Pennsylvania!

8. Carl Sewell and Paul B. Brown, *Customers for Life: How to Turn That One-Time Buyer into a Lifetime Customer* (Crown Business, New York, 2002); "Systems, Not Smiles" is Chapter 5.

9. Isadore Sharp, *Four Seasons: The Story of a Business Philosophy* (Portfolio, New York, 2009).

# chapter 8

1. Taylor Guitars, "FAQ," http://www.taylorguitars.com/guitars/reference/faqs_answers.html.

2. Gerry Barker, "Aboard the *Allure of the Sea:* This Ship Is Giant Fun," *Palm Beach Post,* December 1, 2010.

3. Christopher D. Salyers, quoted by Radley Balko, "The Subversive Vending Machine: The Liberatory History of Automated Commerce," *Reason,* June 2010, http://reason.org/news/show/subversive-vending-machine. The book in question is Christopher D. Salyers, *Vending Machines: Coined Consumerism* (Mark Batty Publisher, New York, 2010).

4. Ibid.

5. Bill Price and David Jaffe, *The Best Service Is No Service: How to Liberate Your Customers from Customer Service, Keep Them Happy, and Control Costs* (Jossey-Bass, New York, 2008).

# chapter 9

1. This information is accurate as of publication. Links can change.

2. The official CAPTCHA site: http://www.captcha.net/.

3. TechTarget/Search CIO website, http://searchcio.techtarget.com/definition/Section-508.

# chapter 10

1. Bill Price and David Jaffe, op. cit.

2. Hsieh, op. cit.

3. Bill Price and David Jaffe, op. cit.

4. Here's an easy-to-follow one-page introduction to Seligman's theory of learned helplessness: http://www.noogenesis.com/malama/discouragement/helplessness.html.

5. Henry Fountain, "When Warnings Don't Work," *New York Times,* May 29, 2011, Week in Review, p. 1.

6. Elizabeth Weise, "Apps Light Up as Skies Darken," *USA Today,* May 31, 2011, http://www.usatoday.com/NEWS/usaedition/2011-05-31-stormapps27-ST-The-rash-of-torn_ST_U.htm.

7. Seth Godin, "Permission Marketing," *Seth's Blog* (blog), January 31, 2008, http://sethgodin.typepad.com/seths_blog/2008/01/permission-mark.html.

8. Quoted from a page in Amazon.com's account management section.

9. Ibid.

10. Peter Shankman, *Customer Service: New Rules for a Social Media World* (Que, Indianapolis, 2011).

11. Bill Price and David Jaffe, op. cit.

# chapter 11

1. National Public Radio, "Fresh Air with Terry Gross," broadcast February 16, 2011.

2. (And if nobody tells you, it's a sign that you have no friends.)

# chapter 12

1. California Coastal Records Project, http://www.californiacoastline.org/.

2. Yelp.com. Emphases are mine. I have altered details of posting, including name of restaurant and some of the food details to avoid adding fuel to the situation.

# chapter 13

1. "Hyatts Face Protests After Layoffs in Boston Area," *New York Times,* September 24, 2009. Also see "Governor Threatens a Hyatt Boycott," *Boston Globe,* September 24, 2009; "Hundreds Attend Rally for Fired Hyatt Housekeepers—Politicians Urge Boycott of the Hotel," *Boston Globe,* September 18, 2009; and the "Hyatt 100" site: http://www.hotelworkersrising.org/hyatt100/.

2. Sarah J. F. Braley, "Cambridge, Mass., Bans Hotels from Outsourcing Housekeepers," *Meetings and Conventions,* October 26, 2011, http://www.meetings-conventions.com/articles/cambridge-mass-bans-hotels-from-outsourcing-housekeepers/c44318.aspx.

3. Spencer Soper, *The Morning Call,* September 27, 2011, p. A1, http://articles.mcall.com/2011-09-17/news/mc-allentown-amazon-complaints-20110917_1_warehouse-workers-heat-stress-brutal-heat.

4. Amazon.com letter to OSHA: http://www.scribd.com/doc/65227130/Amazon-Letter-to-OSHA.

5. Personal correspondence with Tom Caramanico.

6. Randall Stross, "Consumer Complaints Made Easy. Maybe Too Easy," *New York Times,* May 29, 2011, Business section, p. 3.

7. Heather Armstrong, "Containing a Capital Letter or Two," *Dooce* (blog), August 28, 2009, http://dooce.com/2009/08/28/containing-capital-letter-or-two.

# index